The Gold of the pharaohs

The Gold of the pharaohs

Henri Stierlin

·TERRAIL·

Editors: Jean-Claude Dubost and Jean-François Gonthier
English Translation: Peter Snowdon
Cover design: Gérard Lo Monaco and Laurent Gudin
Graphic Design: Sibylle de Fischer
Typesetting and Filmsetting: D.V. Arts Graphiques, 28700 Francourville
Lithography: Litho Service T. Zamboni, Verona

English edition, copyright © 1997
World copyright © FINEST S.A. / ÉDITIONS PIERRE TERRAIL, PARIS 1993
Pierre Terrail/Finest S.A.
A subsidiary of the Book Department
of Bayard Presse S.A.
ISBN: 2-87939-117-2
Printed in Italy

**Pectoral-talisman of Sesostris III
(1900 BC)**

This elegant pectoral, only 5 cm (2 in) high,
is a masterpiece of Egyptian goldwork: the
reverse shows the royal cartouche flanked
by two griffons wearing plumed ostrich-feather
head-dress. (The front is illustrated on page 11).
(Egyptian Museum, Cairo.)

CONTENTS

Introduction: The Flesh of the Gods 9

Discovering Tutankhamun 21

The techniques of the goldsmith
 in Egyptian history 71

Treasures of the Middle Kingdom
 and of the Ramessides 93

Tanis revisited 139

Late-period goldwork: from Pinudjem
 to the Ptolemies 197

Conclusion 211

Further reading 215

Map 217

Glossary 218

Plans 220

Outline chronology 222

Acknowledgements 224

INTRODUCTION
THE FLESH OF THE GODS

This detail from the golden naos demonstrates both the artistic elegance and the tender intimacy that characterize the decoration of all Tutankhamun's treasure. Here, the queen Ankhesenamun hands an arrow to the young pharaoh out hunting.
See pages 21, 28, 29, 32 and 39.
(Egyptian Museum, Cairo.)

Since ancient times, the civilisation of the Nile valley has exercised an irresistible fascination over all those who have come into contact with it. They have been captivated both by its wisdom and by its fabulous wealth, as revealed in the treasures of its rulers and the extraordinary tombs in which they were buried.

Such untold riches have also attracted thieves, grave-robbers and other illicit explorers. Lured on by the promise of easy pickings and the shimmering prospect of precious silver and gold, they forced their way to the heart of even the best protected tombs – those hidden at the centre of the pyramids, in the galleries that ran beneath the Theban hills, buried under the sands of the desert or concealed in the clefts of a cliff.

What drew them there was not just the market value of the objects they hoped to find. Gold has always been considered the

Opposite

Tutankhamun's gold mask, decorated with enamel and precious stones

Although Tutankhamun's tomb was discovered in 1922, the splendour of his treasure only became fully apparent three years later. First, the three funerary "chapels" built of gilded cedarwood had to be opened. Then the heavy lid of the pink granite sarcophagus was lifted revealing two coffins of gold-plated wood, followed by a third coffin of solid gold. Only then did the excavators come face to face with the pharaoh's mask, an astonishing work in polished gold set with multicoloured stones. (Egyptian Museum, Cairo.)

Opposite

**A symphony of colours:
a pectoral of Sesostris III**

Enlarged three times in the
photograph, this Middle
Kingdom pectoral proclaims
the power of the pharaoh,
symbolized by griffons.
The mythical beasts are
trampling negro and asiatic
enemies of the king underfoot.
They are protected by
the goddess Nekhbet, who
appears as a vulture with her
wings outspread, representing
the sky.
(Egyptian Museum, Cairo.)

Following pages

**The goddess Hathor
presenting a necklace
to the pharaoh Sethos I**

Detail of a drawing made in
c. 1820 by Ippolito Rosellini
in the tomb of Sethos I in the
Valley of the Kings at Thebes.
It illustrates the role played
by jewelry in the funerary ritual.
The goddess presents
her necklace-cum-talisman
to the pharaoh, who wears
a bracelet on his wrist decorated
with protective wedjat eyes.
Below, the cartouches
of Sethos I, who ruled in around
1310 BC. The ensemble from
which this detail is extracted
is reproduced on p. 125.

most noble, as well as the most expensive of materials. And the
most beautiful jewels, the most precious talismans and the finest
statues of the gods were all fashioned out of gold.

The ancient Egyptians valued gold in much the same way
that we value art. They prized it less for its intrinsic worth,
than for its many virtues – religious, mythical and symbolic. The
way in which it resisted the changes which time imposed on other
substances came to represent the immunity to corruption of the
gods themselves. Gold does not tarnish, nor can it rust. It persists
unscathed by the passage of centuries, and by atmospheric variations. Thus men desired it as the symbol of survival and eternity,
which they summed up in a simple phrase: "Gold is the flesh
of the gods".

The pharaohs surrounded themselves with treasures, not out
of greed, but because they believed the proximity of gold could
confer on them a sort of eternity. In the great royal hypogea
of the Valley of the Kings, the burial chamber was known as
the sovereign's "Room of Gold" or "House of Gold", where he
dwelled in the afterlife. His coffin too was made out of gold, as
was the death mask. The function of the mask was to fix for all
time the radiant features of the pharaoh who, in being born
again, had become one with the stars.

Both the beautiful goddess Hathor and the radiant Isis, patron
of the dead who, ressuscitated, have taken their place in the
beyond, were seen as embodying this power of gold. Like the sun
which reappeared each morning after having sunk into the
underworld, gold gave man the power to return to life. Thus the
amulets and talismans which were used in rituals to conjure eternity were made from gold. They would be placed in the tomb,
there to perform their alchemy. Gold was also used for the jewelry
and ornaments which were intended to protect the deceased
during the perilous journey through Hades.

Any study, therefore, of the goldwork of the pharaohs must
explore beyond its use in the jewelry of the living and the
brilliant frivolities of ornamental art, to investigate the funda-
mental cultural role it played in Egyptian civilization. For gold
was the object of a veritable cult, which stemmed from the religious significance with which the metal was endowed. Its use by
the dead was a privilege reserved for the high-born, and served
as an emblem of their power. The pharaoh, the divine ruler,
was considered to be "golden Horus" incarnate, son of Osiris.
The insignia he wore were intended to identify him with the
gods. Thus, for example, the golden uraeus – the protective
cobra that rears up over his forehead – was reputed to possess
supernatural power, and was identified with the burning eye of
Ra, the Sun.

This book presents many of the purest masterpieces of Egyptian art, and seeks to explain the spiritual and cultural attitudes that presided over their creation. In doing so, I hope it will bring the reader closer to the way of thinking and the spiritual aspirations of those men and women who inhabited the valley of the Nile thirty or forty centuries ago.

Court rituals and funerary rites

The outstanding works of the goldsmith's art during the pharaonic period present us with a striking image both of the daily life of the ruling classes and of their beliefs concerning the afterlife. The jewels of gold and precious stone that have survived bear witness not only to a refined and lavish art, but also to a constant preoccupation with obtaining some form of protection, both on this earth and in the grave beyond, against harmful forces, such as the "evil eye", that lie in store for human beings.

This need for active talismans, for good-luck charms, for magic amulets, is one of the leitmotivs of Egyptian culture. Jewels are not merely ornaments, however magnificent their appearance may be. They are endowed with a protective function which is part of their intrinsic value. Indeed, in the ritual of embalming and in the funerary impedimenta of the mummy, this function assumes priority over all others.

Thus the ornamental themes adopted were dictated by this function, and acquired a precise meaning. Pectorals took the form of a temple facade or a naos, so that the sacred character of their motifs could not be mistaken. These motifs might be a scarab beetle, the symbol of Khopri, a vulture, symbol of Nekhbet, the solar barque, or gods such as Amun, Hathor, Isis or Nephthys. Sometimes texts from the Book of the Dead were inscribed alongside these figures.

In the early days of the pharaonic culture, the predominant function of these objects may have been to assert, through their splendour, the power of the royal house . The designs of certain famous pieces dating from the Middle Kingdom suggest a conspicuous display of force, as befits an authoritarian monarchy. The motif of prisoners being sacrificed recurs over and over again and is found up until the time of Ahmose, though the final example features, significantly, on a ceremonial axe. It is, however, almost entirely absent from the art of the reign of Tutankhamun, whose favourite profane subjects were hunting scenes. Nor is it to be found in the art of Tanis, which is entirely dedicated to an intense religiosity.

As with most of the crafts practised in ancient Egypt, the techniques used for working gold made relatively little progress over three thousand years. Under the Middle Kingdom, they had already reached their peak of development. Perhaps it is merely

the lack of comparative evidence from the Old Kingdom which prevents us from situating Egypt's "golden age" even further back than 2000 BC.

Yet this lack of technical progress did not prevent a considerable degree of stylistic variation over time. Each of the periods for which we possess a significant number of pieces clearly had its own particular way of fashioning jewelry. It is even possible to distinguish stylistically between individual dynasties.

In the final analysis, despite the gaps in our knowledge, both art lover and historian can find an admirable introduction to Egyptian art in the work of the pharaohs' goldsmiths. These were marvellously talented craftsmen, constantly striving after perfection. The objects they created are both things of beauty and occasions for meditation. In the midst of so much splendour, they never lost sight of the mystical message they were intended to convey. In their work, the "flesh of the gods" is no longer an intellectual proposition, but a concrete reality.

Only in Egypt do we find these shimmering masses of gold and coloured stones, these masks and coffins carved out of precious metals, these gilded naos which glimmer in the depths of hidden sanctuaries. No other culture has bequeathed to us such a magnificent heritage, not even that of the Incas, which was swiftly plundered by the European invaders, its riches melted down to satisfy their greed.

Human memory has tended to identify ancient Egypt as a whole with the "Fields of Iaru" which prefigure the Christian vision of paradise. On every side, the visitor is surrounded by chapels and statues covered in gold leaf, heavy ritual ornaments and ornate liturgical plate, tombs overflowing with incalculable

A small lion, once part of a bracelet of the pharaoh Ahmose

The jewelry of Ahmose, founder of the XVIIIth dynasty in c. 1580 BC, was discovered in the coffin of his mother Ahhotep, whose treasure was rescued for posterity amidst scenes of stirring adventure.
See pages 108 to 115, 118 and 119.
(Musée du Louvre, Paris.)

Opposite

The pharaoh Psusennes I of Tanis

The superb profile is set off by the nemes headcloth and the guardian cobra (uraeus) on the pharaoh's forehead. This mask of beaten but unpolished gold dates from c. 1000 BC. Enamel details are used sparingly to highlight the eyes, eyebrows, and the cord linking the head-dress to the false beard. The discovery of this piece on 28 February 1940 was a major landmark in Egyptian archaeology, equivalent in many respects to the unearthing of Tutankhamun's tomb.
(Egyptian Museum, Cairo.)

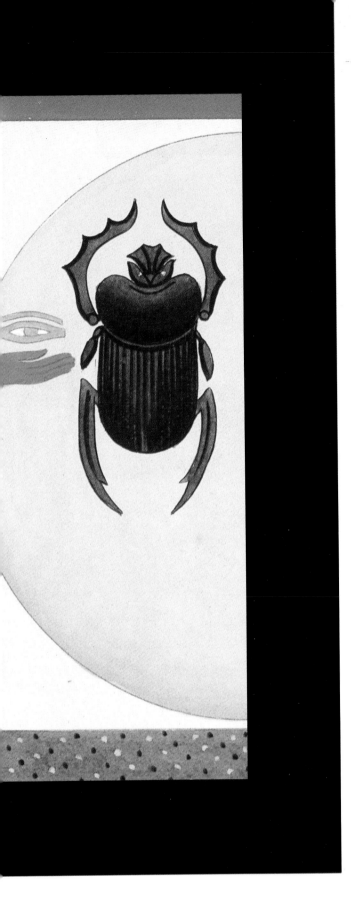

A gold-mounted green feldspar "heart" scarab

Originally from the treasure of one of the Ramessides, this amulet, either
stolen or inherited, was found at Tanis in the tomb of Psusennes I's general,
Wendjebauendjed, placed on the chest of the mummy.
(Egyptian Museum, Cairo.)

Opposite

Ramesses X worshipping the scarab beetle Khopri

As the symbol of the rising sun, and of the resurrection of the dead,
this insect played an important role in Egyptian religious thought. Drawing
(after a painting in the tomb of Ramesses X in the Valley of the Kings) made
in c. 1820 by Rosellini.

Opposite

**Hathor, goddess of dance
and joy**

Hathor is wearing the emblem
of the solar disk between
the horns of a cow, and a calotte
in the form of a heavenly
vulture. She has a broad gorget
on her breast, and bracelets
on her upper arms. Bas relief
from a column in the Ptolemaic
temple at Kom Ombo,
in Upper Egypt.

riches. At every step, we are reminded of the enormous value and significance that was attached to gold – this dazzling and immutable metal, which foretold an afterlife suffused with light flowing from the eternal sun of the resurrection.

Gold is absolutely central to all this splendour. It bears the indelible mark of the gods. It is the symbol of a transfiguration, a blazing halo of light, that preserves the people of the valley and their pharaohs in the radiance of their immortality.

Traces of lost magnificence

Most of the objects that have survived down to the present day, whether in isolation or as part of treasure-hoards, are both artistically admirable, and the expression of a fabulous wealth. As such, they form some of the most prized exhibits of the Egyptian Museum in Cairo and of many great museums in Europe and the United States. And yet, paradoxically, most of the objects covering a timespan of over three millennia date from the reigns of minor rulers or little-known periods.

Thus the greatest single collection of Egyptian jewelry is the funerary impedimenta of an obscure, relatively undistinguished pharaoh known as Tutankhamun who died at the age of twenty. He reigned during the transitional period that followed the religious crisis under Amenophis IV, around 1360 BC and therefore his "trousseau" can hardly have been very impressive when compared with those of other pharaohs who wielded much greater power.

The other major discovery that determines our vision of Egyptian goldwork is that of the treasures of Tanis. These date from the reigns of Psusennes I, Amenemipet and Sesonchis II. Specialists refer to this period, starting in the 9th century BC, as the Third Intermediate Period. It is generally regarded as a time when Egypt's fortunes were in decline.

The few surviving remains from the Old Kingdom are sufficient to hint at what must have been lost when the pyramids of Kheops and of Khephren were sacked. Similarly, rulers such as Tuthmosis III, Sethos I or Ramesses II must have amassed riches far in excess of the wildest dreams of young Tutankhamun. The contents of their hypogea are irretrievably lost, among them the supreme achievements of the goldsmiths at work during those years when Egyptian art was at its apotheosis. The scant evidence that has come down to us from the greatest periods of Egypt's power can do no more than provide a faint picture of the splendour of its rulers' way of life.

DISCOVERING
TUTANKHAMUN

*Two scenes executed in repoussé work on gold leaf, from the naos
of Tutankhamun: on the left, the queen presents a sistrum and a necklace
to the king; on the right, Ankhesenamun is offering flowers and precious
ointments to the young sovereign. (Egyptian Museum, Cairo.)*

Without doubt the most sensational find ever made by an archaeologist was the discovery in 1922 of the tomb of Tutankhamun in the Valley of the Kings (Upper Egypt). It took a combination of determination, intuition and systematic research for the archaeologist Howard Carter (1873-1939) and his patron Lord Carnarvon to track down Tutankhamun. When they got there, they realised they had made a truly outstanding discovery: the only tomb of a New Kingdom pharaoh to have survived to the present day with all its treasure intact. It had lain virtually undisturbed for three thousand three hundred years in a corner of the Valley of the Kings where no one had thought of looking.

This great adventure began on the eve of the First World War. Carter had a theory, and he had managed to convince Carnarvon to back him. He believed there was a tomb that had never been excavated in the Valley of the Kings, one which had belonged to

Opposite

**The opening of Tutankhamun's tomb
in 1922**

By late November 1922, the corridor had been cleared and an iron grille put in place to discourage thieves. The excavators were now able to see into the antechamber brimming with extraordinary treasures – beds, cases, furniture, boats, etc. Howard Carter, Lord Carnarvon and the rest of the team could hardly believe their eyes. It was two years, however, before they were able to begin removing the treasure, on 1 November 1924, and this operation in turn was to last several years.

The gods were present in the pharaoh's tomb

Among the accumulation of objects and jewels
which accompanied Tutankhamun on his journey
to the afterworld, the gods were granted a special
place. Their statues in gilded and stuccoed wood
were placed there to sustain the pharaoh's soul:
Sekhmet the lionness, Mamu, Horus Shu, Sokar,
Ptah and others made up a powerful cortège.
This statue of Osiris is wearing a sleek wig, false
beard, and a six-layered gorget.
(Egyptian Museum, Cairo.)

a relatively undistinguished ruler called Tutankhamun who had
reigned during a period of great instability, having come to the
throne shortly after an unprecedented religious crisis had shaken
the Egyptian state to its very core. In around 1370 BC,
Amenophis IV, taking for himself the name of Akhenaten, had
founded a montheistic cult dedicated to the solar disk, Aten, with
himself as its prophet. The life of his successor, Tutankhamun,
had been brief. He had come to the throne in 1354, and had
reigned for only six years. When he died, he was barely twenty.

When he was made pharaoh, Tutankhamun had adopted the
name of Tutankhaten, so we can assume that the Atenian rites
were still being practised at that time. But the people of Egypt
soon returned to the worship of Amun, the tradition of the priests
of Karnak, once the reformer they had despised was dead. The
young ruler then changed his name to Tutankhamun. The old
order had been safely restored.

On the eve of the war

George Herbert, fifth Earl of Carnarvon, was an aristocrat
and a dilettante, with an enormous fortune at his disposal. He
had developed a passion for archaeology, and had retained
Howard Carter as his scientific adviser. Carter having persuaded
him that there was much still to be discovered in the Valley of the
Kings, he applied to the Department of Antiquities in Cairo for a
licence to excavate the site. Gaston Maspéro, the French egyptologist who had succeeded Mariette Pacha, granted him permission, though he did not really believe that anything would come
of it. Carter and Carnarvon planned to commence their explorations in October of the same year.

That year was 1914. On 28 June, the Archduke of Austria was
assassinated in Sarajevo. On 28 July, Austria-Hungary declared
war on Serbia. By early August, Germany had attacked Belgium
and France. Britain took its place beside the French army. In the
space of a few weeks, a whole continent was at war. The murderous
confrontation that ensued was set to continue for several years.

For the British archaeologists in Thebes, excavation was now
out of the question. They would have to wait for better times.
Only in the autumn of 1917, after the allied victory at Verdun,
would Carter finally be able to make a start on the work that he
had been planning so long.

A self-made man

Howard Carter was no run-of-the-mill archeologist. As an
egyptologist, he was largely self-taught. His fascination with the

Ptah performing "the erection of the djed pillar"

According to an ancient myth concerning stability and the permanence of power, the god Ptah, to whom the town of Memphis was consecrated, was regarded as the patron of goldsmiths. With both hands, he holds upright the djed pillar, crowned with the key of life. Mummy-like, he is tightly wrapped in a shroud of golden plumage and wears a blue faience head-piece and a large magic gorget. Height: 52.8 cm (20¼ in). (Egyptian Museum, Cairo.)

**A gold falcon discovered
in Tutankhamun's tomb**

This superb falcon represents
Sokar, a funerary god who
was also the symbol of metal-
founders. He accompanied
the deceased and watched over
the tomb. This detail shows
the stylized feathers and the fine
blue motif representing
the patch around the falcon's
eye. The stuccoed-wood
sculpture is covered with fine
gold leaf no thicker than
1/200th of a millimetre
(1/5000th of an inch).
(Egyptian Museum, Cairo.)

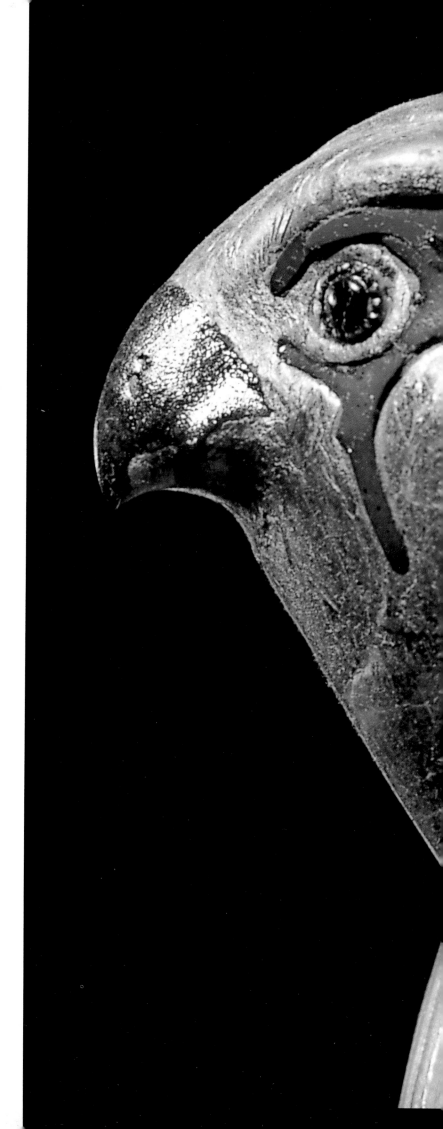

Statue of the fearsome lionness-goddess Sekhmet

Another effigy in gilded and stuccoed wood, this time of the goddess of fury, scourge of the enemies of the sun. The head of a lionness on the body of a woman is intended to inspire fear. Over her head looms the solar disk. She is one of the guardians of the tomb. Sekhmet had her sanctuary in the temple of Mut, at Karnak.
(Egyptian Museum, Cairo.)

civilisation of Ancient Egypt had begun when he was still a child. His first career was as a draughtsman, and it was in this role that he came to work with Percy Newberry at the Egyptian Museum in Cairo. This turned out to be an excellent form of training, especially the time he spent as assistant to two of the leading figures in the profession, the great archaeologist Flinders Petrie and his Swiss colleague, Edouard Naville. Carter learned to decipher hieroglyphs. His skills were noticed and, in 1899, Maspéro appointed him Director of Ancient Monuments for Upper Egypt.

Unfortunately, he only held the post for four years. A fight broke out on the site of Saqqara. Carter was deemed to have been the instigator, but refused to make a formal apology and was stripped of his functions. For the next four years, he hung around on the sidelines of archaeology until Maspéro recommended him to Carnarvon, who was looking for an adviser. In 1906, Carter undertook his first excavation for his new employer.

An American archaeologist, Theodore Davis, had held a concession in the Valley of the Kings since 1902. In 1912, Carter learned that Davis would not be renewing his permit, and he persuaded his patron to apply to take it over. For years, Carter had been studying every aspect of this famous site, where the greatest pharaohs of the New Kingdom had been buried with great pomp and circumstance, during the period between 1600 and 1100 BC. The Valley lies beneath the Western Mountain, behind the great Theban funerary temples opposite Karnak. Carter had reason to believe that it had not yet yielded up all its secrets.

He had reviewed all the investigations that had been carried out since the eighteenth century into the royal hypogea in the Valley. He knew the excavations of the archaeological pioneers – Belzoni the Italian, and the German, Lepsius – inside out. He had scoured everything that had ever been published by the dozens of people who had dug there. He had searched out every trace of the finds made by unauthorised local treasure-hunters, such as the Abd el Rasul clan, who in 1875 had discovered the secret cache known as Deir el Bahari where the remains of around forty pharaohs were hidden. These mummies had been the victims of grave-robbers operating in around 1100 BC. What was left of them had been piously assembled and transported here for safe-keeping by priests at the end of the XXth dynasty.

Carter had drawn up meticulous lists of all the pharaohs and the tombs which they had occupied. He had catalogued every find and every excavation, and identified the origins of all the isolated objects that were scattered between different collections. He knew everything that had been attempted in this field, and all that had been achieved. He also knew that his predecessor in the Valley of the Kings, Davis, had recently found not only the tomb

Anubis, god of the dead and guardian of the necropolis

Carter found the black desert dog in Tutankhamun's tomb seated on top
of a gilded naos in the form of a pylon. His collar and ears are gilded,
and his enamel eyes gaze out onto eternity. This photograph by Harry Burton,
taken just after the discovery, is itself an historical document.
(Egyptian Museum, Cairo.)

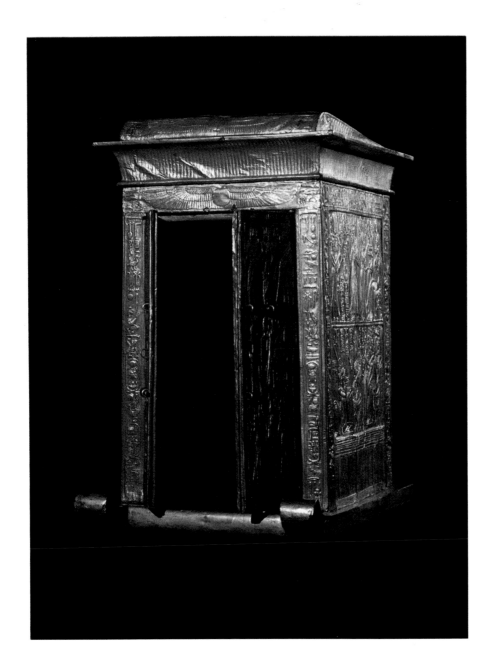

The golden naos from the tomb of Tutankhamun

This "tabernacle" must once have contained a statue of the king-become-god in solid gold, stolen when the tomb was first pillaged in c. 1300 BC. It takes the form of a miniature building with a vaulted roof and a cavetto cornice. It is covered with a thick layer of gold leaf, and stands on silver runners. Height: 50 cm (19½ in); width: 26.5 cm (10½ in); depth: (12½ in) 32 cm. (Egyptian Museum, Cairo.)

Opposite

This repoussé work decoration from one side of the naos shows, in the top compartment, the king standing in a skiff surrounded by rushes. Together with the queen, he is setting off to hunt birds in the papyrus thickets. On the right, he is portrayed wearing the Blue Crown, and is apparently taking his leave of the young Ankhesenamun. In the lower compartment, the king is sitting on a folding chair, while the queen hands him an arrow. (Egyptian Museum, Cairo.)

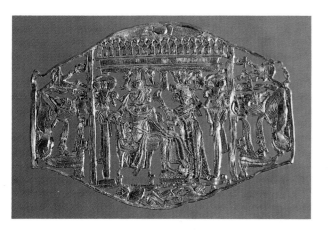

**Tutankhamun on his throne
in the presence of Ankhesenamun**

This delicate piece of openwork filigree gold
(apparently made using the cire perdue method)
shows the king sitting on his throne
while the queen stands in front attending
to him. Width: 8.5 cm (3½ in).
(Egyptian Museum, Cairo.)

Opposite

**A scene in the Amarna style
from the back of a gold throne**

The same theme as on the small jewel above,
now inflated to decorate the back of a sumptuous
throne. Gold and silver reliefs with details
in glass and precious stone depict an intimate
scene: the pharaoh, dressed in ceremonial
costume, nonchalantly leaning against the back
of his chair, receives signs of affection from his
queen. Between the two figures can be glimpsed
the hands in which the sun's rays terminate.
This is a characteristic feature of the Amarna
period and the rites of the Disk, as is the lively,
spontaneous style.
(Egyptian Museum, Cairo.)

of Yuya and Thuya, which contained furniture belonging to
Amenophis III, but also a cache of vases and a small chest bearing the name of Tutankhamun. In 1908 he had discussed the
matter with his colleague Herbert Winlock, assistant curator at
the Metropolitan Museum of Art in New York, and Winlock had
demonstrated to him that these objects must have been those
which were used when the young pharaoh was embalmed.

Carter harboured no doubts. There was a further royal tomb
that had not yet been discovered – that of Tutankhamun.
Perhaps it had been sacked by ancient thieves, perhaps it had
survived intact. Whatever the case, until it was found there
remained the likelihood of a major discovery being made in the
Valley of the Kings. It was this argument that convinced him that
he should carry out a systematic investigation of this rocky desert
site, where the arid atmosphere, the craggy landscape and the
scorching sun that beats down on the royal tombs all conspire to
make men feel that they are close to eternity.

However, despite their enthusiasm, the two Britons had to wait
for the hostilities to subside. Only when the war of the trenches
in northern France had come to an end could they finally set out
in search of the treasure of the little-known pharaoh.

Disappointments and fresh hopes

It is not my intention here to relate in detail the work which
led up to the discovery of Tutankhamun's tomb in 1922. Many
books have been written on the subject, beginning with Carter's
own account. Instead, I shall simply remind the reader of the
main stages in the resurrection of an obscure pharaoh who now
enjoys the sort of fame which even the mightiest of kings can
only dream about.

Perhaps the most striking feature of Carter's investigations was
the single-minded confidence with which he persevered through
five unsuccessful campaigns. His conviction was underpinned by
a series of rigorously logical deductions. He had worked out that
Tutankhamun's tomb must lie within a triangular zone covering
roughly two acres, the apexes of which were defined by the hypogea of Ramesses VI, Merenptah and Ramesses II. So as to ensure
that no stone would be left unturned his team, then had to clear
away the piles of rubble that had been left behind by earlier
archaeologists dig down through the gravel as far as the solid
rock. The work was back-breaking, and generally unrewarding.

Five years were spent shifting hundreds of tons of aluvium and
rock, to little purpose. Right at the beginning, one discovery was
made: the bases of a small number of huts which had probably
housed labourers working on the tomb of Ramesses VI. Then, for

two long years, nothing. In 1919, they came upon some alabaster vases dating from the reigns of Ramesses II and his successor, Merenptah. Then, once more, nothing, until 1921.

Carter's team had begun to doubt his judgement. Even Lord Carnarvon was showing signs of impatience; he thought they should shift their investigations to another site, and was considering giving up his concession. In this state of mind, he decided that the 1922 campaign should be the last. But Carter was still as confident as ever. As he wrote: "My conviction is that as long as there is a single scrap of ground left unexplored, it is worth our while to persevere".

Carter found himself facing a second walled-up door. He had a small opening made in this wall, through which he was able to pass first a candle, and then his head: "At first, I was unable to make anything out, since the warm draught of air from the tomb made the flame flicker. Then as my eyes grew accustomed to the darkness, I saw emerge from the shadows strange animals, statues and gold. Everywhere I looked there was the glow of gold".

He decided to enlarge the opening. As the explorers peered into the underground chamber, they found themselves confronted by treasures on all sides, extraordinary masterpieces piled up in total disorder, as if hastily abandoned. Scattered higgledy-piggledy around the chamber lay beds and trunks, gilded sculptures and chariot wheels, boxes, and stacks of chairs. Those present could scarcely believe their eyes and must have wished but for one thing: to force their way into the chamber brimming with unimaginable treasure.

Scientific method, however, dictated otherwise. Accordingly, they resealed the hole and fixed a solid iron grille in front of the first door while they prepared the next stage of their investigations. Carter had already estimated that it would take months, perhaps even years, to remove and restore all that he had seen. And he did not know then that three other chambers awaited him, each of them crammed full of treasures and votive offerings, each of them richer and more astonishing than its predecessor. The reality that Carter had discovered was soon to surpass his wildest dreams.

Breaking and entering?

But did Carter really have no idea of the scale of the task that lay ahead of him, as he was later to claim? According to Thomas Hoving, who led the team that organised the first exhibition of the treasures of Tutankhamun at the Metropolitan Museum of Art in New York in 1976, Carter possessed less self-restraint than he wished the world to believe. Hoving's hypothesis is that the four leading figures – Carter, Lord Carnarvon, his daughter Evelyne, and Callender, an English archaeologist who had been sent to assist with the opening of the tomb – were so impatient that they deliberately broke one of the cardinal rules of their profession. Together, they entered the tomb on that very first evening, by drilling a "robber's hole" in the walled-up door of the funerary chamber which led to the treasure room. From there they could enter the lateral chamber through an opening which the priests of the necropolis had apparently forgotten to seal off again after the tomb had been pillaged.

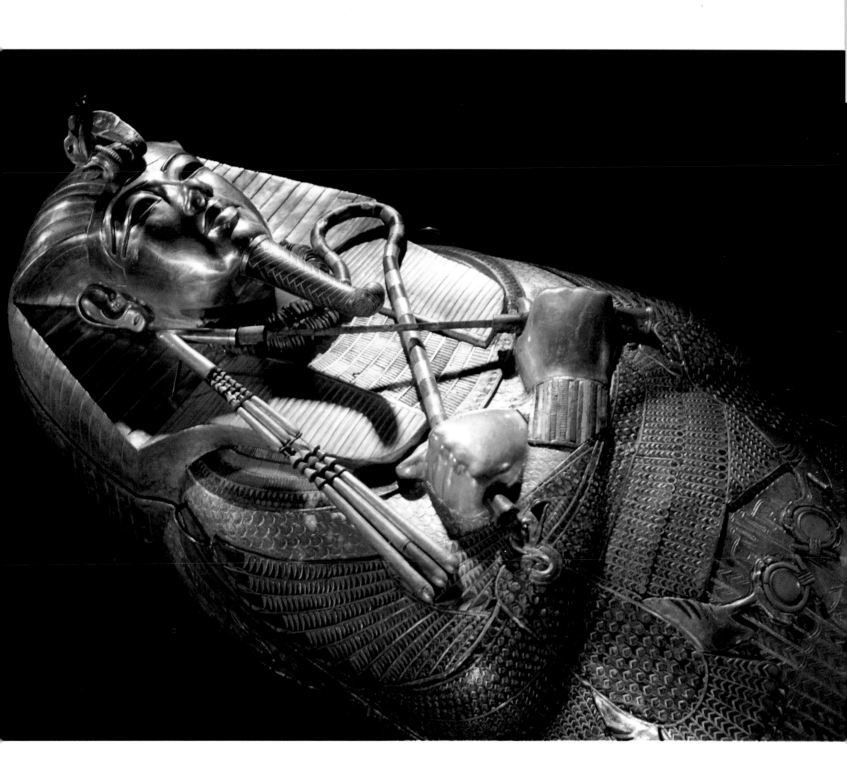

The private life of the royal couple

Two further scenes of the royal couple from
the gold naos.
Above: Ankhesenamun carefully places
a necklace round the neck of the young king
as he relaxes, his elbow propped against the back
of his seat. The queen is wearing a long dress
of pleated linen, of a kind that was fashionable
among Egyptian royalty.
Opposite: Tutankhamun, wearing the Blue
Crown, pours perfume into the cupped hand
of his wife, who is sitting nonchalantly
on a pouffe at his feet. The faintly hieratic style
of the figures is, again, indicative of Amarnan
influence.
(Egyptian Museum, Cairo.)

Hoving's hypothesis is not at all implausible, given the excitement the archaeologists must have felt on discovering the tomb. However, he does not explain how the four ring-leaders escaped the attention of the Inspector of Antiquities, Ibrahim Effendi, an Egyptian bureaucrat, who had been sent out to oversee the opening of the tomb in the absence of his superior, Rex Engelbach, who was held up in Qena.

During these years, Europe was in a state of upheaval, but ominous news of events from overseas had little impact on the workers at the camp in the Valley of the Kings. On 28 October 1922, Mussolini declared his "march on Rome" and, on 25 November, was granted full power to form a government.

Lord Carnarvon died on 5 April of the following year. Howard Carter arrived back in Cairo on 1 October, but work on the site could not resume until agreement had been reached on a new concession.

Accordingly, inventory and conservation work only began on 1 November 1924. There was no lack of things to be done. The first task was to make a start on the burial chamber and the treasure room.

One surprise after another

Whatever the date on which Carter first visited the other rooms in the tomb of Tutankhamun, we can imagine the astonishment he must have felt. Once a stone in the northern wall of the antechamber had been removed, he could see, scarcely a foot away, a surface covered with gold and blue enamel. When the walled-up door was finally opened, Carter realised that he was about to enter the burial chamber, in which a gilded "chapel" had been erected to contain the sarcophagus. This chapel took up almost all the available space, leaving only a 50 cm (19½ in) gap on each side, in a room that measured 6,4 × 4 m (21 × 13 feet).

What he did not know then was that this wooden construction contained another similar, slightly smaller structure, which in turn contained a third, again built on the same model. These three golden envelopes sat one inside the other like a set of Russian dolls, shielding the sarcophagus from prying eyes.

This room held a further surprise for Carter, which he would discover only much later: a sarcophagus of pink quartzite, decorated with the carved figures of guardian goddesses and containing a series of mummiform coffins. The first, in gilded wood, represented the figure of Osiris, god of the dead, and was inlaid with coloured faience and glass fragments. It was opened on 10 October 1925, revealing a second mummiform coffin, this time in gold-plated wood with polychrome details.

Inside this second coffin lay yet a third, bearing a radiant face. Made of a solid gold skin 2.5-3.5 mm (1-1⅜ in) thick and weighing more than 110 kilogrammes (242 lb), it was an object of priceless value. Within this seventh protective envelope, they finally reached the mummy itself with its pure gold mask of mesmerising beauty. Even to this day, the serene expression of contentment and of kindness that radiates from its eyes exerts a magical fascination over all those who behold it.

The canopic chamber

Continuing his inspection of the tomb, Carter then discovered a strange and rather magnificent tabernacle located to the east of the burial chamber, containing the canopic vases in which the entrails of the pharaoh were preserved. This chest was a sort of square vertical chapel, each surface of which had been gilded. Above the central tabernacle was a dais, decorated with a frieze of uraei (cobras bearing the disk of the sun) standing guard over its precious contents. A second frieze of smaller cobras ran round the top of the chest.

On each side of this magnificent structure stood a statue in gilded wood depicting a marvellous goddess figure. All four were dressed in sheath dresses with large openings for the arms and faced inwards towards the centre of the tabernacle, which they vigilantly guarded. Each had a distinct hairstyle, and could be identified respectively as Isis, Nephtys, Neith and Selkis. In their elegance and beauty, they are one of the most moving examples of ancient Egyptian art.

Once again, the floor of the room was strewn with jewelry cases, boxes of games and model boats. A huge black desert hound representing Anubis, draped in a shroud, sat enthroned on a chest which was equipped with carrying bars for processions. A gilded cow's head representing the goddess Hathor was topped off by tall horns in the shape of a lyre. Altogether, there were more than 5,000 objects. It took ten years to photograph them, ensure they were in condition to be transported, and then ship them to the Egyptian Museum in Cairo.

Ancient robbery

From the very outset, Carter was aware that the tomb of Tutankhamun had not entirely escaped the attention of the grave-robbers. This was evident from the openings which the thieves had made and which the priests who looked after the necropolis had carefully sealed up again. Further clues inside the tomb led him to believe there had been at least two attempted

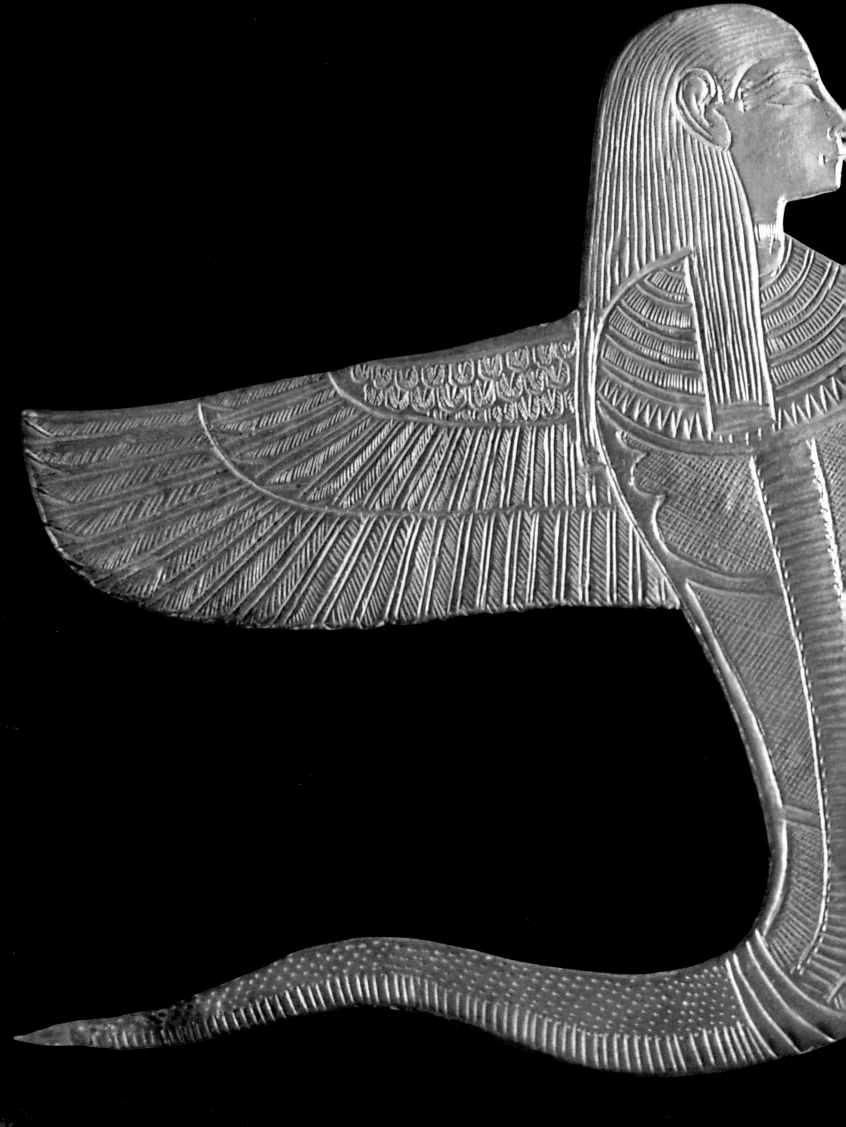

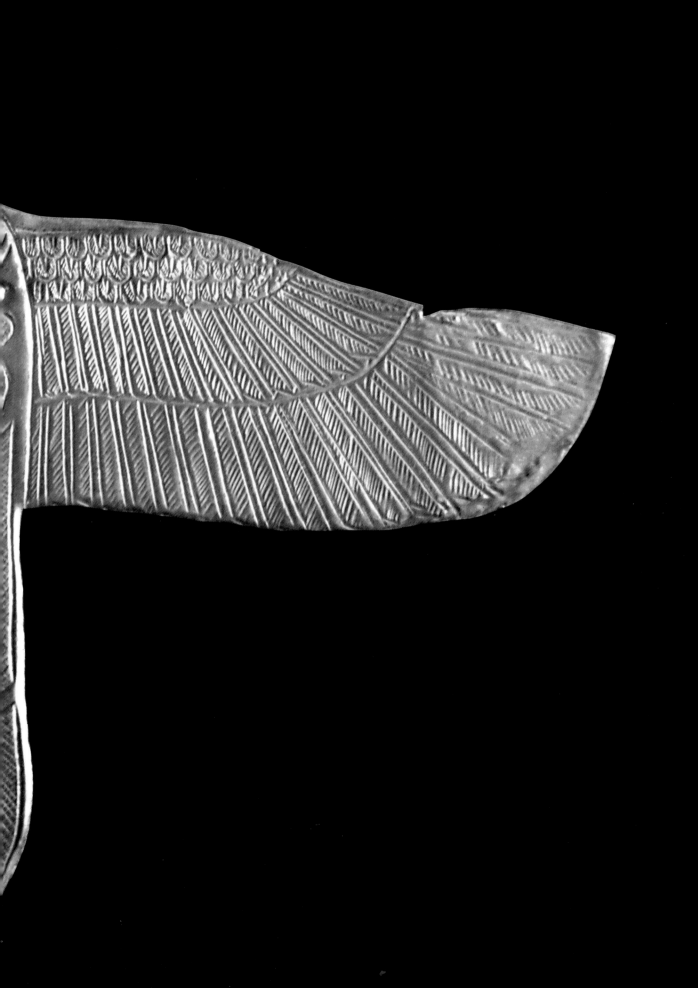

Tutankhamun's flabellum, or fly-swat

This object, which played a key role in pharaonic ritual, is made of gold,
and features both repoussé and chasing. The long gilded handle culminates
in an elegant papyrus umbel. The semi-circular wooden core could hold up
to thirty ostrich feathers in a fan, as can be seen in the drawings of Rosellini.
The back (opposite) depicts the pharaoh's triumphant return from the hunt,
with two servants carrying his kill; the front (above) shows him in full pursuit
of a group of ostriches. Width: 18.5 cm (7½ in). (Egyptian Museum, Cairo.)

49

Ointment box of Tutankhamun in the form of cartouches

The sides of the box feature gold repoussé work reliefs of the divine
guardian (the god of eternity), above whom appears the winged scarab,
Khopri. The pharaonic cartouches are crowned by the solar disk.

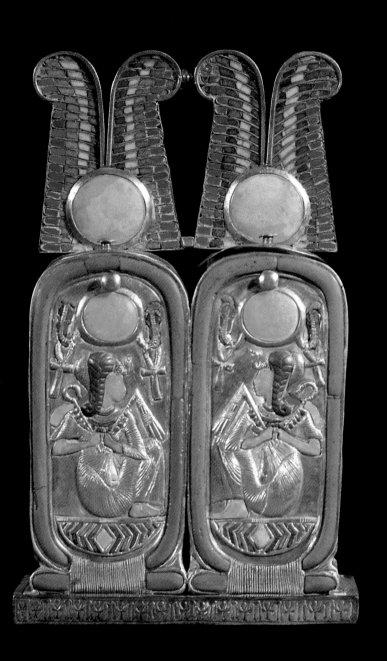

This superb piece of goldwork must have formed part of the ritual apparatus for the funeral ceremony. It is 16 cm (6¼ in) high, including the feathers sprouting from above the solar disk. Instead of the names of the king, each cartouche contains an image of the crouching pharaoh. On the right, he wears the blue crown; on the left, the traditional tress of the royal children. This outstanding piece, with its gold relief designs, lapis lazuli and cornaline inlays, and silver base, is a major achievement of ancient Egyptian art.
(Egyptian Museum, Cairo.)

**Dagger with gold blade
and handle decorated
with granulations**

Decorated with cloisonné
bands made of precious stones
and coloured glass alternating
with granulated motifs, this
golden dagger – an example
of consummate craftsmanship –
was found in the coffin
of Tutankhamun. The sheath
(above, and detail opposite)
depicts bulls and ibex being
pursued by lions, leopards
and dogs. Length: 32 cm
(12¹/₂ in); sheath: 21 cm
(8¹/₄ in).
(Egyptian Museum, Cairo.)

one of mutual consideration and charm. On the back of the gold throne with its silver and enamel highlights, in between the images of the two sovereigns appears the sun, its rays culminating in so many hands – an image typical of the Amarna period and of the cult of the Disk. In some of the cartouches, the pharaoh is even given the Aten form of his name: Tutankhaten.

A similar scene from courtly life is to be found on a jewel of solid gold with an openwork design, decorated with granules. On this tiny object, the king is depicted seated on his throne while the queen stands before him, stroking his hand as she offers him a bouquet of lotus flowers.

His sceptre is of an unusual design, decorated with enamel bouquets of papyri and sacrificial scenes in repoussé work. A text alludes to the cult of the Disk: "the beautiful god, the beloved whose face shines like Aten". This phrase is accompanied by the name of Tutankhamun, thus proving once again that this is a work from a transitional period.

Among the instruments and emblems of power is a large fly-swat, which would have been decorated with ostrich feathers. On the front face of the semi-circle that forms its centre, is a scene depicting the pharaoh hunting ostriches. At that time, such birds must still have been found on the edge of the desert. He stands alone in his war chariot, taking aim with his bow and arrow, while a hound flushes out a pair of the birds. The reverse side of this fine object depicts the homeward-bound Tutankhamun with two porters carrying the game he has bagged.

The two daggers found in the tomb were not intended for war but for the hunt. Hunting was a noble pastime, and the expression of a royal prerogative. The superb finish of these two

Tutankhamun's ritual sceptre and daggers

Centre, detail of the handle of the dagger illustrated on pages 52-53.
Left and right, front and back of the royal sceptre, decorated with scenes
of animal sacrifices. The chased repoussé work on the latter should be
compared with the alternating granulations and coloured cloisonné work
of the former. Length of handle: 11.8 cm (4¾ in).

The king's iron-bladed dagger

Left, the 54 cm (21¼ in)-long sceptre, with
its rod culminating in a papyrus umbel. Right,
a second dagger belonging to Tutankhamun.
Exceptionally for the period, it has an iron blade.
By 1300 BC, the use of iron in the Nile Valley
was still extremely rare and this piece must
therefore have been even more precious than
the gold-bladed dagger. The granulated
decorations of the handle are to be compared
to those on the previous dagger (pages 52-53,
and detail page 54). The pommel is made
of quartz while the sheath is covered
with fleur-de-lys motifs within a twisted cord
surround on the front, and with a plumage
motif on the back.
(Egyptian Museum, Cairo.)

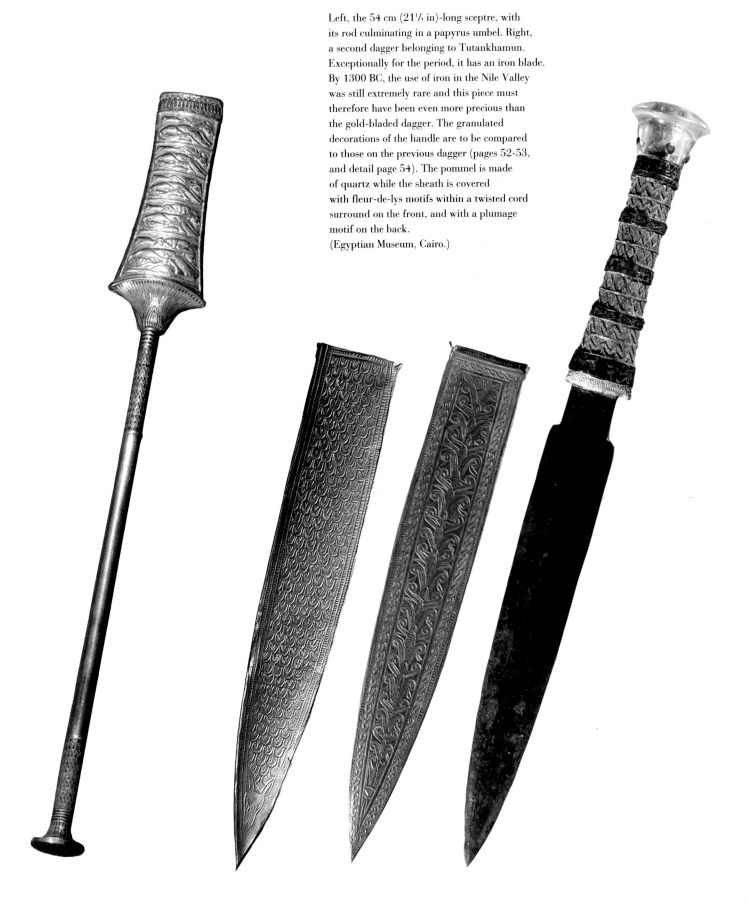

A minuscule crouching figure of the pharaoh

This solid gold pendant reiterates the motif of the pharaoh as a child wearing
his war helmet (see page 51). Standing 5.4 cm (2⅛ in) high, it was found
inside a box bearing the name of queen Tiy, the wife of Amenophis III.
(Egyptian Museum, Cairo.)

pieces – and in particular the repoussé work hunting imagery on one of the two sheaves, showing dogs and wild animals bringing down ibex and bulls – identifies them as ceremonial objects. The handles are decorated with granules, terminating in a knob of quartz. The blades, however, are of iron. The precious nature of these pieces is also indicated by the fact that they were found on the mummy of the pharaoh himself.

Tutankhamun's tomb contained hundreds of finely-crafted gold objects. One of these is especially symbolic: a precious ointment box, in the form of a double royal cartouche. This wonderful object is made of gold and decorated with cloisonné work in coloured stones. It shows the pharaoh as a child, seated. He can be identified by the long tress of hair hanging down from the crown of his head on the reverse side, and, on the front, by his warrior's helmet. Both sides feature the figure of the god of eternity, surrounded by the names of the king, and surmounted by a scarab beetle symbolising Khopri, the rising sun.

Thus, among the "provisions" that the pharaoh took with him on his journey, goldwork was everywhere at hand, whether he was sitting on his throne or out hunting with his dogs, displaying the insignia of power or conducting the ceremonies of state.

The pharaoh's jewels

Jewelry is, of course, the primary domain in which the goldsmith can give the full measure of his art. Tutankhamun's jewels are no exception to this rule. They encapsulate the achievements of the royal jewellers active at the end of the XVIIIth dynasty (around 1350 BC). For the Egyptians, this apparently frivolous genre was no mere luxury, as we have already remarked. Jewels had a religious function: they were intended to protect the wearer, both in life and in death.

Talismans were just as important in the afterlife as in the present, if not more so. The perils to be met in the next world, as enumerated in religious texts such as the *Book of Portals*, or the *Book of what is in the Underworld*, were far more threatening than anything to be found in this world. The deceased would therefore have need of all the protective devices available.

That is why bracelets, rings, necklaces, ear rings and pectorals often represent symbolic figures drawn from Egyptian mythology. They are amulets, endowed with a magical power, through their emblems of life, strength and eternity. Among the most common active symbols to be used were Khopri the scarab beetle, the cobra-uraeus, the guardian wedjat eye, the vulture of the goddess Nekhbet, Horus the falcon, Sekhmet the lionness, and the beautiful goddesses Isis and Nephtys.

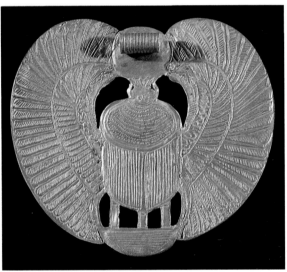

A magnificent pectoral in the form of a scarab

This protective pendant was found in a box along with several other admirable pieces. With its remarkably harmonious form it offers a perfect example of the way New Kingdom goldsmiths mounted coloured stones in cloisonné work. A lapis lazuli scarab spreads out its wings in a circle, the wing-tips clasping a red cornaline solar disk. The representation of the large quill feathers forming a fan-like composition is a virtuoso display of craftsmanship. Height: 9 cm (3½ in). (Egyptian Museum, Cairo.)

A pectoral in the form of a falcon with outspread wings

This talisman features an elegant composition. In a rigorously symmetrical design (excepting the leftward-facing golden head), the sun bird is depicted with its wings spread out in a broad circle, its multi-coloured plumage expressed by meticulous cloisonné work in lapis lalzuli, cornaline and blue glass. Height: 12.6 cm (5 in). (Egyptian Museum, Cairo.)

Reverse of the sun bird, treated in chased gold

The back of the cloisonné matches the polychrome front surface in sheer
beauty. The restrained decoration, relying purely on chasing, offers a perfect
foil to the radiant splendour of the gold itself. Four clapper-rings have been
added, allowing the pectoral to be hung in such a way that the gold chain does
not detract from its contour. This falcon is probably not Horus, who was
worshipped at Edfu, but Ra-Horakhty, the god of Heliopolis, represented
in his relation to the solar myth.

Opposite

Two ear-rings worn by the pharaoh

Ear-rings for men became fashionable under
the reign of Akhenaten, through the influence
of the Asiatic kingdoms. These magnificent
articulated pieces are wonders of minute
and precise detail. Beneath the pin, intended
for a pierced ear, a bird fans out its wings
in a circle, in the centre of which appears
a tiny blue-glass head with its black eye.
Five free-hanging chains decorated with enamel
chevrons terminate in miniature uraei.
Diameter: 5.2 cm (2 in); height: 10.9 cm (4¼ in).
(Egyptian Museum, Cairo.)

Two signet rings belonging to Tutankhamun

Tutankhamun was found wearing several rings.
Those pictured above are in solid gold; the flat
surface is engraved with images of the gods.
On the right, Ra-Horakhty, Horus of the Horizon;
on the left, Amun, indicative of the restoration
of the Theban cult in the aftermath
of the Amarna heresy.
(Egyptian Museum, Cairo.)

Among those jewels that survived the pillage of the tomb were
those worn by the mummy, who escaped intact in his sarcophagus, protected by the chapels of gilded wood. These alone make
up one hundred and forty three pieces, most of them of a very
high quality. Nor were they all specially created for the dead
king's entombment, for as the Egyptologist Jean Capart has
observed, "these jewels show slight but unmistakeable signs of
wear, which prove that they were actually worn by the young
pharaoh".

Nor are these jewels all endowed with a religious significance.
Some of them are merely beautiful, and often very simple. Their
only function was to satisfy the pharaoh's vanity and taste for
ostentatious luxury. Accordingly, some bracelets, whether broad-
banded or slim, are simply decorated with coloured strips of
inlaid stone – lapis lazuli, turquoise and cornelian in the tradition of certain pieces found in the tombs of the relatives of
Tuthmosis III. Such jewelry was particularly suited to be worn by
the pharaoh when he set off to wage war.

Other bracelets are more elaborate. One shows a fine, highly
stylised wedjat eye, featuring a design of great purity. Another is
crowned by a simple veined green stone, framed by granular
motifs and surrounded by milled decorations.

The bracelets regarded as real talismans were ornamented
with scarab beetles, as an invocation to the god Khopri, the symbol of the rising sun and thus of eternal return and resurrection.
One such bracelet, with a large lapis lazuli scarab relief, is one of
the finest goldwork objects in the tomb of Tutankhamun. The
artist fashioned the insect's body, legs and pincers out of a single
piece of solid gold. The sense of detail and of observation is
remarkable and the entire bracelet is perfectly finished, even
down to the borders of coloured stone.

The rings found in the tomb are often very simple signet rings
of solid gold, in which are engraved images of the god Amun
enthroned, or of Ra-Horakhty (Horus of the Horizon) with his
falcon's head. The images are inscribed on a surface which takes
the form of a cartouche, for the rings also served as seals. They
seem to have been associated with the restoration of the cult of
Amun, after the heretical interlude of Tell el-Amarna.

The number of ear-rings found in the tomb of Tutankhamun
may come as a surprise. It would seem that male ear-rings
became fashionable during the time of Akhenaten. One of the
finest pairs is an astonishing feat of miniature cloisonné work. Its
principal theme is a bird with multi-coloured wings spread out in
a circle. The head is a piece of translucent blue glass which has
been worked down to the finest detail. In its claws the bird holds
the symbol of infinity. Beneath hang a series of small chains

An astonishing range of bracelets

On the left, an ornamental bracelet of the most
restrained kind: a rigid ring of gold decorated
with lapis lazuli. On the right, a large articulated
two-part bracelet. The hinge sits opposite
the pin-operated clasp. This design, with bands
of gold and precious stones, is known from
earlier periods, thanks to pieces belonging
to the wives of Tuthmosis III (1450), himself
an ancestor of Tutankhamun.
(Egyptian Museum, Cairo.)

The mummy and his bracelets

Representing a wedjat eye, held to possess protective properties, this articulated bracelet was found on the right arm of the pharaoh. The stylised eye, with its human eyebrow and falcon-inspired motif beneath (Horus was the golden eye of the sun), is a constantly recurring theme in Egyptian art. (Egyptian Museum, Cairo.)

This articulated bracelet, with a pale stone surrounded by fine granules, was found on the left arm of the pharaoh. There is no talismanic symbol. The bunched papyrus shoots are the only figurative element. Tutankhamun's mummy was discovered wearing seven bracelets on his right arm and six on his left.
(Egyptian Museum, Cairo.)

This bracelet was probably the most magnificent in the king's possession. It was found in a fine cartouche-shaped box, which also contained earrings (see page 61). It is decorated with a magnificent scarab sculpted out of lapis lazuli and representing Khopri, the rising sun. The legs and pincers are of solid gold, set between polychrome borders featuring floral motifs. (Egyptian Museum, Cairo.)

63

Pectorals: jewelry as protection

Many pectorals were found among the jewelry of Tutankhamun, most commonly designed in the form of the facade of a naos or temple – a trapezoid frame surmounted by a cavetto cornice. Opposite and on this page, above, the back and front of a piece which combines several different talisman functions. In the middle is the djed pillar, an ancient "totemic" symbol of stability and permanence, on top of which sits the solar disk. On either side are cobras wearing the crowns of Lower and Upper Egypt, their tails leaning against the royal cartouches. Beyond them are the goddesses Neith and Isis, standing with their wings stretched out in a protective gesture.
Height: 12 cm (4¾ in); width: 16 cm (6¼ in).
(Egyptian Museum, Cairo.)
Centre and below: a pectoral depicting a vulture, symbol of Nekhbet, the goddess of the sky, with the royal cartouches. As in the previous example, the front features cloisonné work using precious stones, and the back is in chased gold.
Height: 12.1 cm (4¾ in); width: 17.2 cm (6¼ in).
(Egyptian Museum, Cairo.)

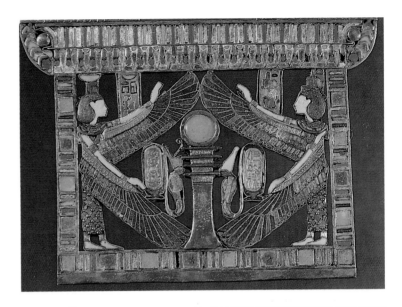

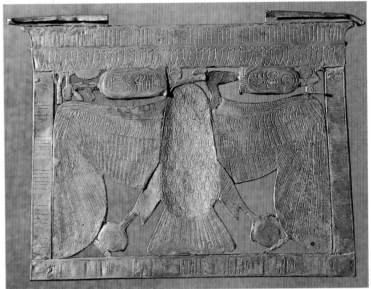

The vulture pectoral: a masterpiece of craftsmanship

This piece, a golden pectoral found on the
mummy of Tutankhamun, is perhaps the most
perfect treatment in any medium of the theme
of the heavenly vulture. The front (above, life
size) is decorated with lapis lazuli and red and
green glass cloisonné work representing the bird's
plumage. The body is treated in relief, and the
head in the round. The eyes are made of obsidian
and the beak of lapis lazuli. The back, opposite,
is three times life-size. Hanging from the bird's
neck is a tiny pectoral, with a cartouche flanked
by two uraei. The inscription is only 5 mm
($^1/_{10}$ th in) high, but nevertheless legible.
Height: 6.5 cm (2½ in); width: 11 cm (4¼ in).
(Egyptian Museum, Cairo.)

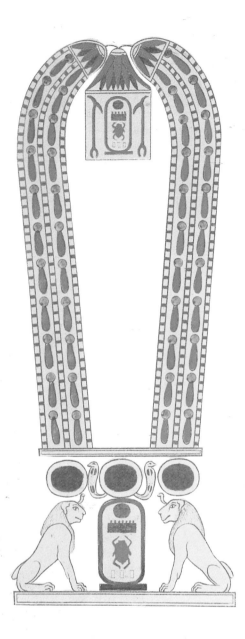

Pectoral necklace with counterpoise

This drawing was made by Rosellini before 1830 in the tomb of Tuthmosis IV in the Valley of the Kings at Thebes. It illustrates the way in which such jewelry was balanced by means of a counterpoise which hung down the pharaoh's back. The counterpoise in the form of a lotus flower is attached to a broad chain made up of several strands. The pectoral shown opposite, representing the lunar bark, similarly features a counterpoise decorated with a lotus flower on both front and back. Below, the image of the moon's nocturnal transit, as it emerges from the primordial swamp. The disk and the crescent are of electrum, the bark iself is in gold. Width: 10.8 cm (4¼ in); counterpoise: 6.8 cm (2¾ in). (Egyptian Museum, Cairo.)

made in polychrome cloisonné, culminating in cobras, whose heads are reared up in the form of the ureaus. Each of these minute snakes is a tiny wonder.

A major sub-category among those jewels which were primarily talismans is that of the pectoral, a complex pendant typical of the gold work of this period. Many superb examples of such pieces have survived from the Middle Kingdom.

The jewelry of Tutankhamun contains examples of all kinds ranging from the most traditional rectangular designs, which imitate the form of a temple facade with its cavetto cornice, to the most freely inventive. In this last group are to be found motifs such as boats, birds, plants or insects, presented independently, without any surrounding frame. This mode of presentation already existed during the XIIth dynasty, in the treasure of the princess Sithathoriunet.

The function of the pectoral as amulet is emphasised by the choice of ornamental theme. In one fine example, in the form of a pylon, the goddesses Isis and Nephtys, appearing as angels *avant la lettre*, have surrounded a djed pillar (symbol of stability and permanence) with their wings; in another, a superb poychrome vulture representing Nekhbet is inscribed in a precise miniature architectural frame.

The same vulture is to be found again, this time without any restricting frame, in an extraordinary cloisonné work pendant. It is difficult to class this work as a pectoral, given the extreme freedom and independence of the bird, which is treated in slight relief, its wings half-open. The perfection with which the lapis lazuli cloisonné work renders the plumage of the body and the large quill feathers of the wings is breathtaking.

In a similar vein, there are two superb pieces representing the falcon Horus and the scarab beetle Khopri, both with their wings opened out to form a circle. Once again, the polychrome cloisonné work is quite superb. These pectorals are among the undisputed masterpieces of the goldwork of the closing years of the XVIIIth dynasty.

Perhaps, to our eyes, some of the other objects may seem either unduly ornate or sentimental. This may be due to the continuing influence of the Amarna style and the excessive liberties which Akhenaten's heresy had encouraged in the domain of the arts. It is, however, precisely this transitional character which makes the work found in the tomb of Tutankhamun so interesting. And no matter how we may judge its artistic merit, there can be no dispute that the goldwork found in the young pharaoh's tomb represents, in purely technical terms, a stunning apotheosis.

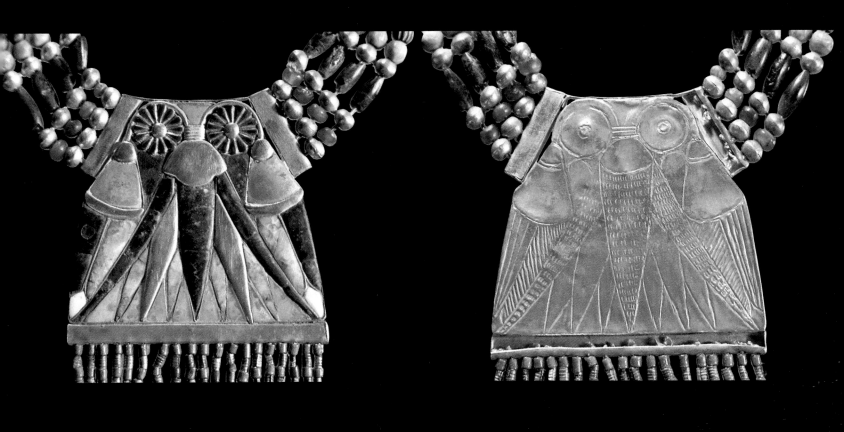
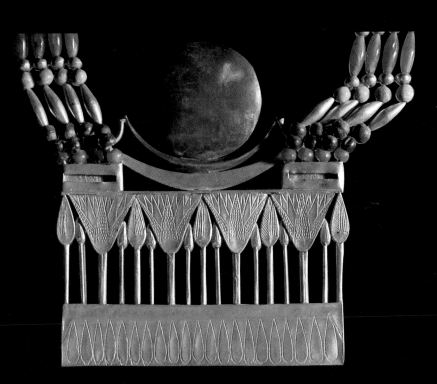

The Techniques of the Goldsmith
in Egyptian History

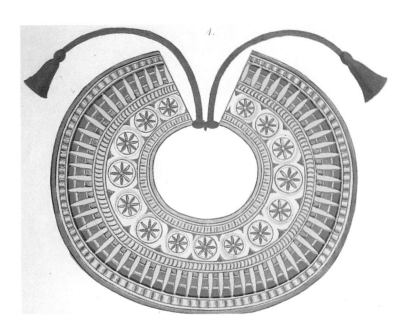

Gorgets, or necklaces with several strands of polychrome beads made
from gold, glass and stones are typical items from the repertoire
of Egyptian jewelry. This drawing by Rosellini depicts such a piece,
with the laces used to attach it.

The treasure of Tutankhamun illustrates the virtuosity of the goldsmiths of Egypt. Delicate jewelry and massive sarcophagi alike testify to the phenomenal level of technical mastery that had been achieved. But how had this mastery been acquired? Working gold is an art that requires a great deal of specialised knowledge and technological skill. How had the Egyptians developed the techniques required to extract the metal from its ore, melt it down, cast and solder it, create alloys and fix its colour?

In this chapter, I want to look more closely at the role played by gold during the pharaonic period by examining the different phases in the development of goldworking technology, in the context of the history of the Nile valley. To this end, I shall describe the different methods employed by the artists and

Opposite

Making gold jewelry

This bas relief from the Old Kingdom dates from the VIth dynasty (c. 2300 BC). It forms part of the decorations of the tomb of the vizier Mereruka at Saqqara and features a series of scenes illustrating ancient metallurgical and goldworking techniques (see pages 76-77, 80-81 and 90-91). This image depicts the weighing of ingots before the metal is cast. The operation is carried out on a twin beam scale. The instrument is held out at arm's-length by the worker, while a scribe records the weights on a tablet.

71

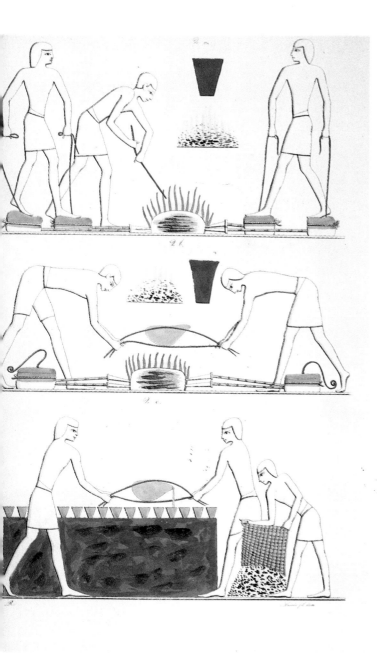

Metallurgists at work

This picture comes from the tomb of Rekhmire
at Sheikh abd el Qurna (XVIIIth dynasty,
c. 1430 BC), after a drawing by Rosellini.
It shows the techniques employed during
the New Kingdom: above, workers fan a fire
by foot-pumping animal skins used as bellows.
By pulling on cords with their hands, they can
refill the empty skins thus ensuring a continuous
supply of oxygen to the fire. In the centre,
workers place a crucible on the fire. Below,
molten metal is poured into moulds.

craftsmen who created these objects of unrivalled perfection.
Anyone who knows a little about the processes of metallurgy,
jewelry-making and enamelling, will find their achievements all
the more astonishing.

The evolution of the techniques of working gold has to be seen
in the context of the overall progress of Egyptian civilisation.
Writing, architecture and metallurgy all made their first appearance at the same time. The sudden and inexplicable emergence
of these three technologies marks the beginning of what we call
history.

When we survey the three thousand-year history of Egypt, its
destiny seems to unfold with all the tranquil power of a great
river. The course of the Nile, on which life in the valley is entirely
dependent, has hardly shifted at all since the beginning of the
Neolithic period, between seven and eight thousand years ago. But
neither before, nor since, has there been a moment of such rapid
technological transformation as that which occurred at the beginning of the pharaonic period. In later years, the pace of innovation
was much slower. Since artistic forms seem to have been fixed
during the first dynasties, the unattentive observer might easily
overlook the continuing evolution of Egyptian arts and crafts.

This evolution took place within a circumscribed world. Egypt
was in effect an island, stranded amidst the vast deserts that
spread out around it to both east and west. Contact with the out-
side world was possible only to the north and to the south. To the
north lay the delta, increasingly marshy as it stretched towards
the mediterranean coast and for long navigable only with diffi-
culty. The many branches of the Nile served to filter out foreign
shipping; only a few ships trading with Asia could pass through.
To the south lay Nubia (now the Sudan) and Black Africa. In
this direction lay the major trade routes through which Egypt
imported perfumes, slaves, ivory and gold.

The unification of Egypt

The valley of the Nile was unified politically for the first time
in around 3000 BC, under the reign of the legendary King
Narmer who founded the First Dynasty. He wore the double
crown, or pschent, of Lower and Upper Egypt, which combined
the short red cylinder of the Delta with the tall white tiara-like
structure that symbolised the Valley. The Two Lands were thus
joined in a symbiotic relationship which would thereafter be reinforced whenever strong government, rigorous administration and
unchallenged authority prevailed.

Any weakening of central government, however, or destabilisa-
tion of the royal house owing to internal strife or foreign invasion

brought renewed schism, division and fragmentation and the re-emergence of two distinct realms. In the north, the kingdoms of the Delta would regroup around their own capital in Lower Egypt. The south would often be split up again into feudal principalities scattered along the length of the valley. None of these local powers, however, ever seriously challenged Thebes as the capital of the region.

The Egyptian "miracle"

During the first three dynasties, between c. 3000 and c. 2650 BC, Egypt evolved into a country through a series of miraculous leaps forward. On every front there was rapid progress and startling innovation. Efforts were made to control the land and adapt it to agricultural use. To combat the annual Nile floods, an extensive programme of works was undertaken. Villages were built on specially constructed levees beyond the flood line; dykes and irrigation canals were created. Such activities required a disciplined workforce under the control of a central authority. That authority was created by instituting the function of pharaoh, an absolute sovereign who soon came to be regarded as divine. The pharaoh reinforced the stability of the nation, determining its social hierarchy and its political structure. He assumed control over the destiny of what was rapidly becoming a coherent state, and established a powerful administrative apparatus.

At the dawn of Egyptian history, three phenomena emerged simultaneously: a complex form of writing, transcribed by means of hieroglyphs; new stone-working techniques; and new religious practises. The latter were founded on a corpus of existing traditions and myths, which had to be coordinated into a coherent ensemble. In prehistoric times, when the deserts of Libya, the Sahara and the Sinai were formed by a drying-out process that began some ten thousand years ago, the various tribes that converged upon the Nile in search of a new life each brought with them their own customs and beliefs. Political unity, towards which the country was clearly heading, could only be achieved through religious unity. This led the royal clergy to organize the deities of the different traditions into new triadic or enneadic pantheons. Right up to the beginning of the common era, the theologians continued to work at honing this synthesis. Yet, with the exception of the short-lived Amarna heresy (1360 BC), restricted to a small élite, Egyptian polytheism never fully mutated into monotheism.

The first three dynasties also witnessed the emergence of a distinct architectural and artistic idiom. The forms that first appeared at Saqqara under the reign of Djoser (c. 2800 BC) were

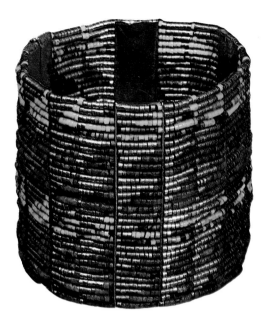

A supple bead bracelet: gold, lapis, turquoise and cornaline

Thirty gold wires are held in place by gold cloisonné work, and the beads are distributed so as to form regular triangular motifs. This bracelet comes from the tomb of Queen Ahhotep at Dra Abul Naga, Thebes and dates from the reign of the pharaoh Ahmose, founder of the New Kingdom, c. 1580 BC. Height: 4.3 cm (1¾ in). (Egyptian Museum, Cairo.)

**Map of the Wadi Hammamat
gold mines**

This 71 cm (28 in)-wide papyrus
document, dating from
the XXth dynasty (c. 1150 BC),
represents the pharaonic gold
mines at Wadi Hammamat,
located in a mountainous region
of the Eastern Desert between
Thebes and the Red Sea. Teams
of slave labourers toiled there
mining gold under extremely
harsh conditions. This is one
of the oldest known maps
in the world.
(Museo Egizio, Turin.)

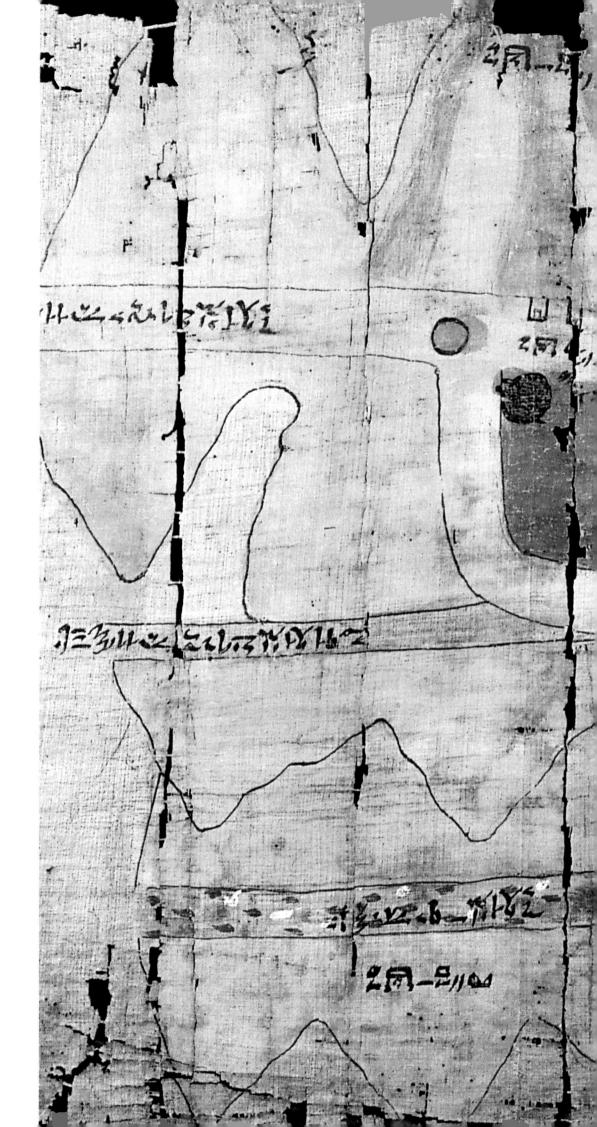

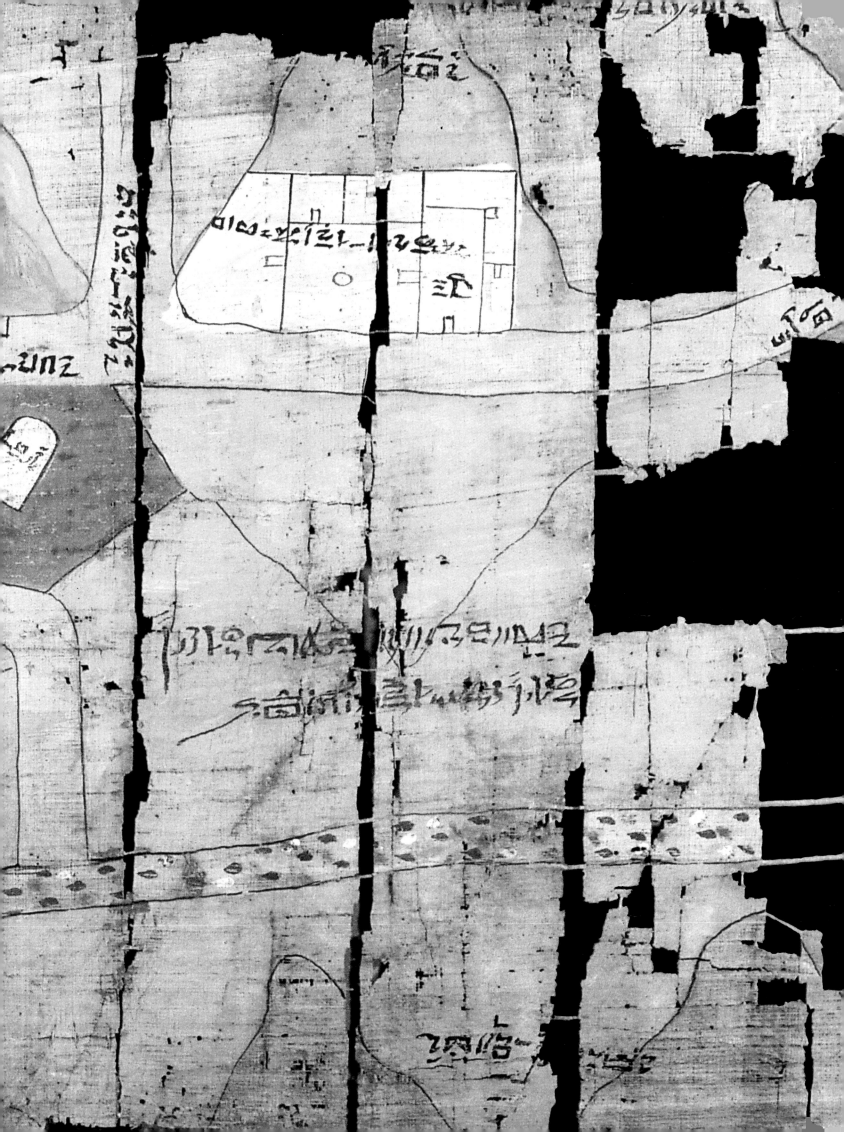

to survive, more or less intact, to the very end of the pharaonic era. The statuary and bas reliefs of this period already display the conventions which would dominate funerary monuments, temples and royal palaces throughout three millennia.

A three-stage itinerary

Historians have divided the evolution of Egyptian civilization into three major phases, separated by dramatic episodes of upheaval, invasion and cultural collapse; they thus refer to three great "Kingdoms" and three "Intermediate Periods".

1. The Old Kingdom encompasses the period from the IVth to the VIth dynasty, between 2700 and 2250 BC. This was an age of prosperity – the age of the great pyramids. It was followed by a period of instability – the First Intermediate Period – which lasted for almost two hundred years, marked by insurrections and popular uprisings. In this revolutionary atmosphere, royal

Two dwarves presenting a necklace on a table

This bas relief from the mastaba of Mereruka at Saqqara depicts, with almost caricatural vivacity, dwarf goldworkers. As in Black Africa, metallurgical trades (blacksmiths, goldsmiths etc.) were often carried out by hunchbacks or dwarves, commonly believed to be invested with magical powers.

tombs and the mastabas (graves) of the nobility were sacked, and banditry was rife.

2. The Middle Kingdom, which comprises the XIth and XIIth dynasties, lasted from c. 2040 to c.1780. It was the period of classical perfection in Egyptian civilisation. This "golden age" came to an end when the country was invaded by the Hyksos, a Canaanite people who first steadily moved into the Delta, then ultimately took control of all of Lower Egypt in the course of the Second Intermediate Period. Their reign lasted through the XVth, XVIth and XVIIth dynasties, i.e. from 1750 to 1580 BC.

3. The New Kingdom commenced when the Hyksos were defeated by Kamosis, whose brother Ahmose went on to found the XVIIIth dynasty. This was the glorious age of pharaonic conquest. Between 1550 and 1100, when the XXth dynasty came to an end, Egypt was at the peak of her power, save for a brief collapse following the religious crisis provoked by Akhenaten in around 1360. Following the brilliant reigns of Sethos I and

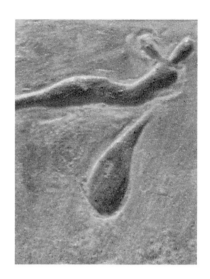

Offering of sistrums and necklaces to a deceased couple

This tomb painting, recorded by Rosellini, shows a deceased couple receiving gilded bronze sistrums and items of jewelry from their servants. A table laden with flowers, fruit and poultry will ensure that they have all they need to eat in the afterlife. Musical instruments, particularly sistrums, are emblems of Hathor, the goddess of joy and sacred dance, and are often included among the funerary provisions.

Ramesses II, the Ramesside era was one of gradual decline, leading to a Third Intermediate Period, during which the country was frequently torn by internal strife.

The Late Period which followed nevertheless lasted for more than 1500 years. From the XXIst dynasty, whose capital was at Tanis in the Delta, to the XXIIIrd dynasty (i.e. from c. 1100 to c. 730 BC), the pharaonic civilization managed to survive in a fragmented country. Then came a period of repeated invasions: first the Kushites or "Ethiopians", whose capital was at Napata in the Sudan (713), followed by the Assyrians (671), then the Persians, who seized the country twice (525 and 343), before the arrival of Alexander the Great (332) and his Greeks who founded the Lagide dynasty (305-30 BC). The Greeks were in turn followed by the Romans. The Roman Empire maintained the fiction of native Egyptian sovereignty and emperors wielded power as nominal successors of the pharaohs. The last great temple in which Egyptian priests officiated at Philae was closed in 537 AD by General Narses, who banished the cult of Isis from what was henceforth a Christian country.

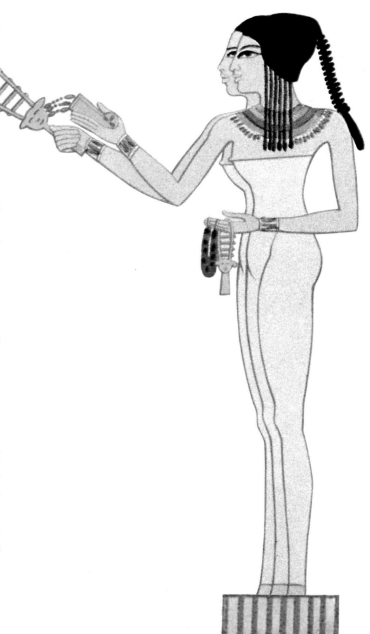

The invention of metallurgy

During the greater part of its history, pharaonic Egypt remained a stone age civilisation. Although this may seem paradoxical, it simply means that while the Egyptians were familiar with metal, they made use of it only in the limited fields of personal ornamentation and religious worship.

The principal tools used in building the pyramids – hammers, beetles, pickaxes, etc. – were made of stone. Blades, punches, scrapers and adzes were fashioned from flint, found in great quantities in the sub-soil of the Nile valley. The Egyptians displayed a remarkable mastery of stone-working technique.

We could, for instance, cite the many beautiful large knives boasting finely-worked blades, such as the knife of Gebel el-Arak, an illustration of the art of Nagada, dating from 3500 BC. The virtuosity which the Egyptians had already achieved during the protohistoric period can also be seen in numerous carved stone vases. Tens of thousands of these objects have survived, all of them made without the use of a lathe. Five thousand years ago, their various forms had already been categorised, and classed according to their ritual function. Fashioned both out of the hardest stones – granite, diorite or basalt – and the most beautiful – alabaster or schist – these vases and plates are worthy forerunners of those that would later be cast out of metal.

At the same time as this admirable stone technology was taking shape, the first copper tools appeared, giving rise to what

Old Kingdom dwarf metallurgist

The task of working precious metals was often carried out by the deformed. Such workers, it is said, were easier to identify and supervise. Moreover, given their diminutive legs they were less likely to abscond.

is known as the chalcolithic period, beginning (somewhat hesitantly) in around 4000 BC. While stone was found in abundant variety throughout the valley and the deserts, seams of copper were in comparison quite rare. Although relatively low-grade deposits of copper ore existed in Egypt, in the Arabian desert, the absence of any source of tin delayed the making of bronze until many years later. Thus, excepting the occasional saw blade, copper was used almost exclusively for ceremonial ojects and liturgical vases. It was also employed by sculptors, as was shown by the discovery of a superb copper statue of Pepi I dating from 2200 BC.

The scarcity of the ore does not in itself explain why copper was so little used in making tools and arms. The reason lies rather in the lack of combustible materials in Egypt, where there were neither forests nor trees to produce charcoal in any quantity. As a result, copper was never widely used for making everyday objects. Later on, tin was imported from Asia, making it possible to manufacture bronze weapons, and under the New Kingdom iron also appeared; yet again, and for similar reasons, their use never became widespread. Pharaonic Egypt never became a major producer and consumer of metals for practical purposes.

The banks of the Nile were never lined with smelting works, vast furnaces, huge crucibles or other harbingers of incipient industrialisation. With the sole exception of mines employing slave labour in dreadful conditions, such as that at Wadi Hammamat in Upper Egypt, where a seam of gold had been discovered, "industry" was restricted to craft production carried out by small teams of workers.

The value of gold

In pharaonic Egypt, the value of gold could not be quantified. Save during the Greco-Roman period, money was unknown; courageous soldiers, loyal administrators and meritorious dignitaries were all rewarded in gold, presented by the pharaoh in person to those deemed worthy of official honour.

Moreover, it would seem that from the New Kingdom onwards (around 1500 BC), gold was used as a means of valuation or payment in different kinds of exchange. It served as a standard of fixed value. In an economy based on barter, prices could thus be expressed in relation to a given weight of gold. Stamped ingots of fixed weight were apparently used for major transactions, while for everyday commodities, copper, silver or even sacks of corn or barley were used.

According to the historian François Daumas, the standard for economic exchange was the *kat* which, from the time of the Old

Casting gold under the Old Kingdom

Around a terracotta crucible, six workmen are fanning the flames using long reeds fitted with ceramic nozzles at their lower ends to prevent them from catching alight. They take it in turns to blow air on the fire under the small crucible in which the gold is being melted down. This bas relief from the tomb of Mereruka illustrates the most rudimentary kind of casting technique. Later on, following the introduction of animal skins as bellows, only two workmen were required to "blow" the fire (see page 72).

**The gold falcon
of Hierakonpolis**

The city of Nekhen in Upper
Egypt, later renamed
Hierakonpolis, was the centre
of a prehistoric cult of the falcon
Horus. It is there that in 1898
this magnificent gold sun bird,
with its crown and uraeus and
the twin feathers of Amun-Ra,
was discovered. Made by the
technique of swageing, it was
hammered out of a thick sheet
of gold leaf on a wooden last.
The beak is a separate element
which has been soldered on.
The French goldsmith, Emile
Vernier, has pointed out that
the two eyes are made of a single
bar of obsidian, the rounded
ends of which have been highly
polished. The work dates from
the VIth dynasty (c. 2300 BC),
and is thus one of the earliest
gold sculptures to have survived
to the present day. Height
of the head alone: 10 cm (4 in);
of the uraeus: 5.1 cm (2 in);
of the feathers: 28 cm (11 in).
(Egyptian Museum, Cairo.)

Kingdom, was equivalent to 7.5 grammes of fine gold. The *deben* was worth twelve *kats*, or 90 grammes. During the New Kingdom, silver was adopted as the monetary standard. The XIXth dynasty witnessed the appearance of the *kite*, valued at one tenth of a silver *deben*: 10 bronze or copper *debens* were equivalent to 1 silver *kite*.

Silver was originally very rare in Egypt and, quite literally, worth its weight in gold. However, when supplies began to be imported from Asia, its value dropped sharply and, by the end of the Middle Kingdom, gold was twice as valuable as silver. Moreover, gold often contains a certain proportion of silver, and when this exceeds one-sixth of the total weight, the resulting mixture is known as electrum, an alloy occurring naturally in the Nile valley and which the Egyptians long believed to be a distinct kind of metal.

Rapid advances in the goldsmiths' art

Egyptian metallurgy thus began with gold, and later added silver to its repertoire. We know something of the working methods of the craftsmen who lived four thousand years ago from bas reliefs found in Old Kingdom tombs. One example shows a necklace being made: an ingot being weighed under the observant eye of a scribe; men blowing through ceramic-nozzled rods to fan the flames beneath the crucible; the piece being cast; and finally, the presentation of the finished object.

The invention of bellows represented a major technical breakthrough, as did a novel labour-saving system involving a pair of goat skins attached to the workers' feet: air was pumped out of one skin as the other simultaneously refilled, thus obtaining a continuous supply of oxygen, and, correspondingly, a real increase in temperature.

At the beginning of this century, the French goldsmith Emile Vernier made a technical study of Egyptian jewelry. He catalogued the metals used (gold, silver, electrum), the precious stones (lapis lazuli, carnaline, turquoise, beryl, amethyst, garnet, quartz, obsidian, pearls and amber) and their imitations (glass, or frit, enameled ceramics, etc) which could be produced in various colours: white, blue, yellow, red, green and violet. During the Old Kingdom a rich palette was already available. Vernier was also able to reconstruct the procedures used by the pharaohs' goldsmiths, and to demonstrate the variety of techniques involved. Objects could be assembled by riveting or soldering. As the latter technique requires an alloy with a lower melting-point than that of the pure metal elements to be fused together, gold was commonly soldered using electrum.

The majestic sun bird

This close up – enlarged
to four times life size – shows
the extraordinary perfection of
the workmanship, in particular
around the edge of the eye. The
interplay of surface and volume
is handled with great authority.
(Egyptian Museum, Cairo.)

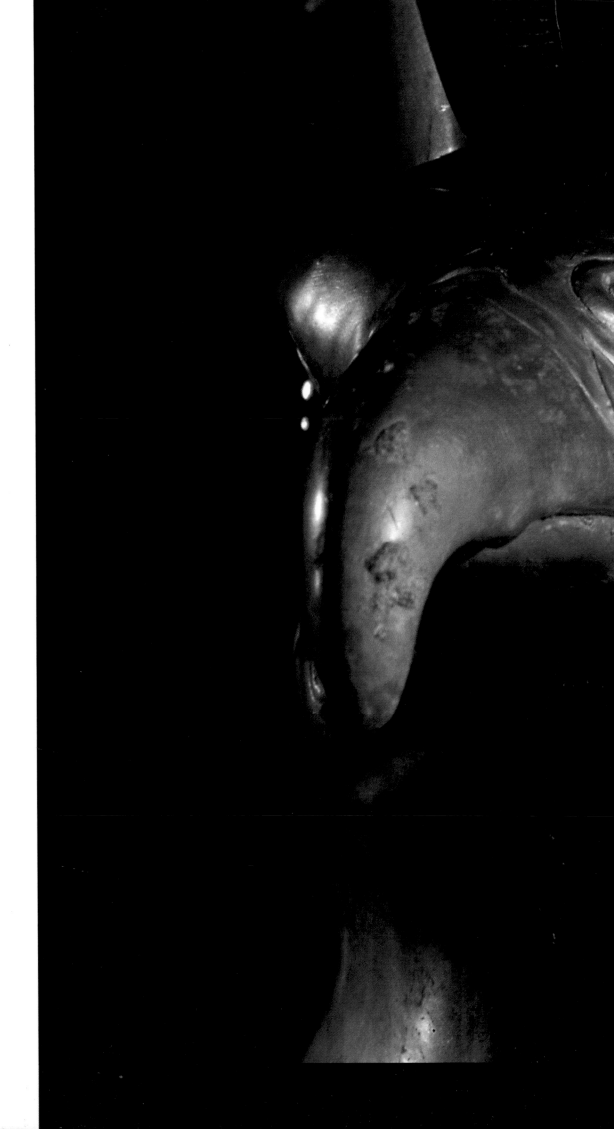

In order to make a container such as a vase, Egyptian craftsmen would use the technique, later adopted by boilermakers, known as swageing. As this involves hammering out the form from a pre-heated sheet of metal, the object being worked upon has to be repeatedly returned to the forge. In the final stages, the gold would be scoured using saltpetre, ammonia or urine, and potassium nitrate to give it a more homogeneous appearance.

Egyptian metalworkers swiftly mastered a whole range of techniques such as mould casting, cloisonné work (embedding coloured stones between fine metal "borders"), filigree, granulation, chasing and repoussé, beating out and inlaying, as well as niello, all of which we will return to later as we examine the objects reproduced in the present book.

Thus, from the very outset, a whole panoply of technical resources was available. With the notable exception of the lathe – a tool which would have enabled certain operations to be performed much more rapidly – the goldsmith and lapidary had at their disposal everything they might need to produce the most magnificent jewelry and ornaments for the pharaoh and his entourage.

Creations in gold

As has already been pointed out in relation to the extraordinary riches found in the tomb of Tutankhamun, the work carried out by the Egyptian goldsmiths was extremely varied in scope. By the time of the New Kingdom, their technical know-how enabled them to produce objects ranging from the smallest amulet, weighing perhaps no more than a few grammes, to massive solid-gold sarcophagi, weighing more than a hundred kilogrammes, along with male and female jewelry, statues of the gods, golden masks, and ritual vessels including cups, ewers, bowls, jugs, goblets, bottles, flasks, chalices and paterai of precious metal. We should also mention the reliefs and sculptures, made in stuccoed wood and covered with gold leaf no more than 1/200th of a millimetre (1/5000th of an inch) thick. This gold leaf technique also featured on the cedarwood chapels encasing the sarcophagi, and which assumed architectural proportions.

Nor should we omit to mention the ceremonial weapons – axes, knives, daggers, clubs and bows – highlighted with solid-gold or similar motifs, and decorated with chasing, reliefs, or even enamel and set stones.

In addition, a whole arsenal of fingerstalls, trusses and pectorals, endowed with magical or propitiatory powers, were produced for funeral rites. Different ceremonies required a variety of offerings, including amulets or talismans, as well as censers and silver tables.

86

Decorated jewelry caskets and chests

If some of the caskets seen in tomb paintings
are very simple, others are just as splendid
as the treasures they contained.
Opposite: certain jewelry boxes have survived
from the Old Kingdom almost intact. This fine
four thousand year-old piece of marquetry
in ivory, blue frit and glass was discovered
in the Gebelein necropolis, north of Thebes.
Height: 19 cm (7½ in).
(Museo Egizio, Turin.)

For the common people, there were lucky charms and bracelets reputedly charged with positive energy. Jewelry was expected to confer benefits both in this world and the next, and the eternal metal, gold, was valued for its intrinsic protective properties.

We should also mention here those objects which have not survived to this day, but which are known to us from tomb paintings: countless items of a symbolic or decorative nature, compositions of great complexity featuring miniature trees made of electrum, animals such as lions, birds or giraffes made out of forged or smelted gold, and even exotic figures – negroes or asiatics – represented in the manner of some engimatic ex voto. Works such as these, which feature in the frescoes of the tombs of Huti, Sebekhotep or Ramesses III, have a peculiarly "baroque" appearance.

Thanks to the work of these craftsmen, the land of Egypt appears in retrospect as a world where "gold is as common as sand on the seashore, as dust on the roads". This magnificence was reflected and magnified in the accounts of countless travellers and invaders, accounts which inspired both the ancient grave-robbers and modern-day archaeologists.

The all-too-rare discoveries of fabulous, perfectly-preserved tombs, whether in the Valley of the Kings or in the necropolises of Lower Egypt, have merely confirmed our image of the splendour of this civilisation; a splendour due above all to the victorious pharaonic armies which brought back precious gold from all parts of the world; from Ethiopia or Nubia, from the mythical land of Punt or from Southern Arabia, Syria or Mesopotamia. And so the rich land of Egypt grew richer on the tribute conquered nations had to pay in order to redeem their debts or buy back their freedom.

**Proud artisans presenting
their finished work**

A bas relief from the tomb
of Mereruka at Saqqara.
Two goldsmiths – a fat master
and his assistant – are showing
off a large necklace. They grip
the laces elegantly between two
fingers to raise their masterpiece
up over the table. Meanwhile,
with their free hands,
they prevent it from swaying
so that the viewer can admire it.

Treasures of the Middle Kingdom and of the Ramessides

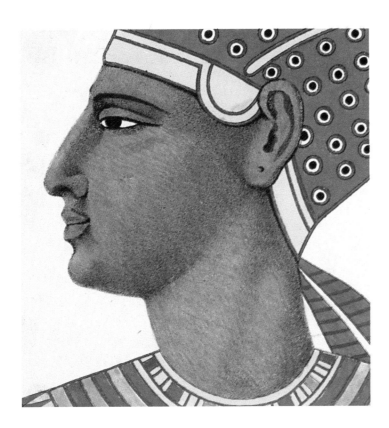

During the New Kingdom, the warrior-pharaohs were not adverse to wearing jewelry (see page 93), as can be seen in this drawing published by Champollion in 1835.

In 1892, a French archaeologist and geologist who had graduated from the Ecole des Mines was appointed director of Egyptian Antiquities in Cairo. His name was Jacques de Morgan. He was a great traveller with an insatiable curiosity and had already visited India, the Caucasus and Persia. In 1894, the same year in which French President Sadi Carnot was assassinated and Dreyfus condemned and sent to Devil's Island, de Morgan launched a major campaign of excavations on a site at Dashur, south of Saqqara. This site was the location of the two enormous pyramids of Snoferu, the first pharaoh of the Old Kingdom (IVth dynasty, c. 2700 BC), and of the remains of several smaller ruined pyramids dating from the Middle Kingdom (c. 1900 BC).

Opposite

Theban tomb painting copied by Richard Lepsius

The German scholar published his first series of such drawings in 1849. This picture shows the importance of head-dresses and jewelry in ancient Egypt: necklaces, diadems and wigs all formed part of the same ideal of beauty and taste for conspicuous display known to us from the tombs of nobles and pharaohs.

**Champollion's copy of a painting
of a pharaoh in his finery**

This king is wearing the blue head-dress, often
referred to as the war helmet. It is made up
of a leather hat, decorated with gold disks and
a gold uraeus, no doubt the reason why it was
among those objects stolen during the first raid
on Tutankhamun's tomb. The pharaoh wears
a multiple-stranded gorget around his neck
and bracelets on his upper arms. Such finery
would have been worn when he officiated
in the temple or when leading his men
into battle.

**Gold necklace in the form of cowrie shells
belonging to Princess Mereret**

This necklace, made up of both small and large
imitation cowrie shells, was found in the Middle
Kingdom tombs discovered at Dashur by Morgan
in 1894. It dates from 1900 BC (XIIth dynasty)
and illustrates the restraint and economy
characteristic of the art of this period when
Egyptian goldwork was at its apogee.
(Egyptian Museum, Cairo.)

A double discovery

Here de Morgan decided to explore a necropolis which surrounded the remains of the pyramid of Sesostris III. In the net-
work of underground tunnels he came upon the king's tomb.
Grave-robbers had been there before him; as he wrote: "It is
common in Egypt for tombs to have been pillaged only a few
years after they were built". He pressed on into a warren of
wells and galleries where there was neither air nor light. Soon, he
realised that he was "no longer in the king's tomb, but in a gallery belonging to two princesses called Sithathor and Mereret,
which leads off the main tomb".

He added that "painstaking examination of the floor of the
galleries revealed, on 6 March, a hollow dug out of the rock at
the foot of the great sarcophagus. The ground here was friable
and the worker's feet went straight through the loose remains.
It needed only a few blows with the pickaxe, and the hiding place
– for such it was – yielded up its treasures: gold and silver jewels
and precious stones were piled up among the wormeaten remains
of the casket in which they had been locked. This cubic box,
originally measuring thirty centimetres (one foot) along each
edge, had been reduced to dust".

De Morgan had stumbled on an astonishing collection of
works. The most remarkable was an extraordinary gold pectoral
set with coloured stones (lapis lazuli, emeralds and cornelian)
each mounted in its own small frame, using the technique
known as cloisonné. The overall form was trapezoid, inspired
by the design of the temple naos. Within this outline, the motifs
had been defined in openwork. Two representations of the
falcon Horus wearing the pschent (the double crown) stood to
either side of a cartouche in which was inscribed the name of
Sesostris II. The rest of the cache was made up of thirty-six different objects – pendants, necklaces, pearls, scarabs, and others.

"The day after this discovery" wrote de Morgan, "we made a
further, even more important find". These were the jewels of the
princess Mereret. "The hiding place, which was much larger than
the preceding one, was similarly located. Like the treasure of the
princess Sithathor, these jewels had been deposited in a casket
inlaid with gold. But there were far more of them, their inscriptions were longer and three royal names appeared on the pectorals, bracelets and scarabs: those of Sesostris II and III, and that
of Amenemhet III". This collection of masterpieces included not
only several outstanding pieces of jewelry, but also a fine silver
mirror, with a handle in the form of a column. At the top, the
column terminated in the emblem of the beautiful goddess
Hathor, identifiable by her bovine ears.

3

S. Cherubini del.

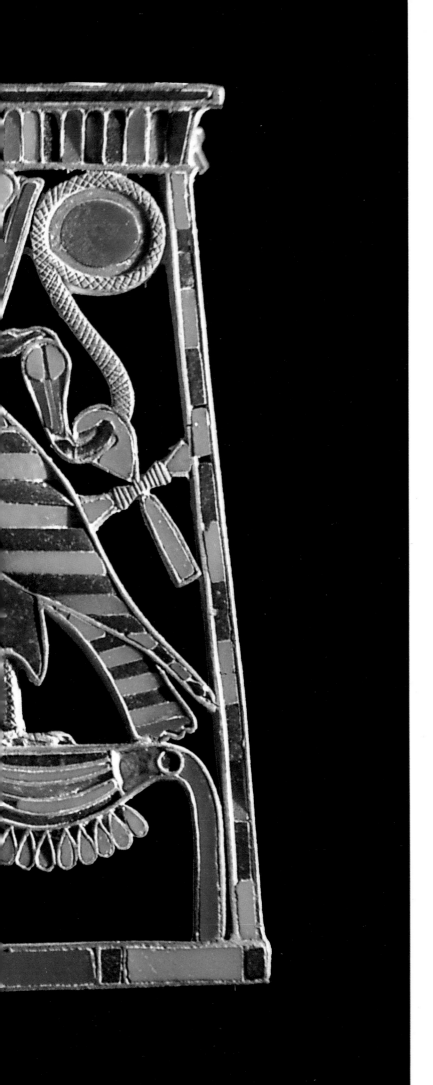

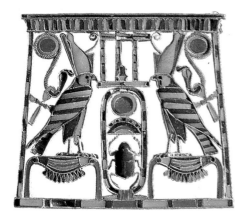

**A sheer masterpiece
from the Middle Kingdom**

This pectoral is perhaps
the finest single example of
artistic genius and refinement
of taste in Egyptian jewelry.
It belonged to the princess
Sithathor. It was discovered
at Dashur by Morgan, and dates
from the reign of the XIIth
dynasty pharaoh Sesostris II
(c. 1900 BC). The frame, in the
form of a naos, is no more than
5.2 cm (2 in) high: the image
above is life-size. In the
reproduction on the left,
the surface area is enlarged
approximately twenty times.
On either side of the royal
cartouche stands a falcon
representing Horus, and wearing
the double crown. In the upper
corners, wrapped around the
sun, are cobras (uraei) from
whose necks dangle the keys
of life. The cloisonné work is
executed in turquoise, lapis
lazuli and cornaline. The fine
open work design is supremely
elegant and illustrates
the Egyptians' indifference
to naturalistic representation:
neither the stripes nor
the colours of the birds' plumage
betray the least sign of realistic
treatment.
(Egyptian Museum, Cairo.)

Amenemhet III massacring prisoners of war

This pectoral was found in the tomb of princess Mereret at Dashur.
It illustrates how jewelry also served to assert pharaohonic power. Within
a trapezoidal frame, representing the facade of a naos, the fine openwork
design combines many different symbols. At the top, the vulture Nekhbet
spreads her wings in representation of the sky. To either side of the royal
cartouches, in a demonstration of royal power, facing images of Amenemhet
III depict the pharaoh, his mace poised ready to strike the prisoner
he is clutching by the hair. The djed pillars beside the raised arms signify
the stability of his kingdom. Width: 10.4 cm (4 in).
(Egyptian Museum, Cairo.)

A marvel in pure gold

The rich harmony of reds, ochres and blues that characterizes the front
of this piece contrasts with the back which is given over to the magnificence
of gold alone. The consummate skill of the craftsmen who fashioned this
object four thousand years ago in Lower Egypt is self-evident. Chasing
was employed to define details too subtle to be captured in cloisonné work.
The uniformity of a single material gives pride of place to line and
composition. (Egyptian Museum, Cairo.)

99

A splendid silver mirror representing the goddess Hathor

This mirror was found at Illahun in 1914 during the excavations carried out by Flinders Petrie and published in 1920 by Guy Brunton. It belonged to a princess of the XIIth dynasty and is made up of a thick disk of silver with a mock papyrus-stalk jasper handle in the form of a curved Hathoric column. The gold cloisonné work is set with lapis lazuli and cornaline. The capital represents the goddess's head, with her bovine ears. Above this motif stands an elegant umbel, the curved gold edge of which echoes the lines of the silver mirror. Height: 28 cm (11 in). The reproduction opposite is approximately life size. (Egyptian Museum, Cairo)

Why had these treasures been stored so far from the sarcophagi and from the tomb proper? De Morgan offered the following explanation: "At the moment of burial, the ancients, quite correctly thinking that one day the treasures piled up in the sarcophagi in the offering chambers and on the mummies themselves might fall prey to thieves, carefully hid these jewels in a place where no one would ever think of looking for them. That is why they had never come to light before".

The royal cobra of Illahun

Another major discovery was made some forty five miles south of Dashur, at the site of Illahun, close to the oasis of Faiyum. This was a region that had been extensively developed by the Middle Kingdom pharaohs, who had drained and irrigated the land around the famous Lake Moeris. In 1920, the British archaeologist Sir Flinders Petrie, who was later to work in Palestine, was excavating the remains of a pyramid. He had only just begun clearing the surface layers, when he came upon a superb uraeus, the rearing cobra that adorned the brows of the pharaohs, ready to strike down their enemies with its piercing gaze.

The ureaus was made of solid gold, set with coloured stones such as garnets and lapis lazuli. The importance of this find, according to Petrie's colleague Guy Brunton who wrote an account of their discovery, lay in the fact that this was the first piece of goldwork that was known for certain to have belonged to a specific pharaoh (in this case, Sesostris II).

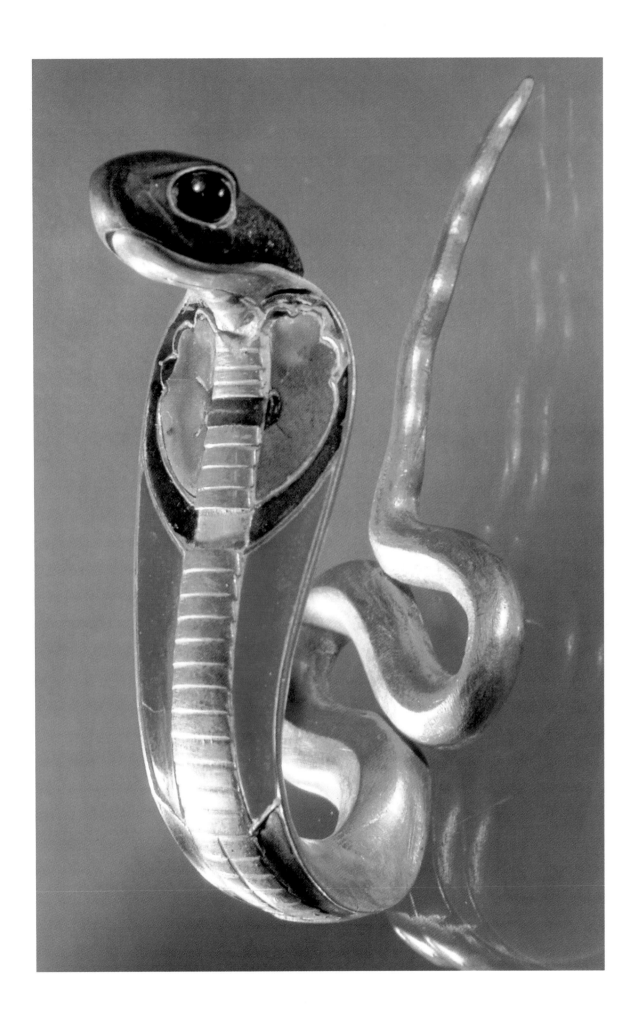

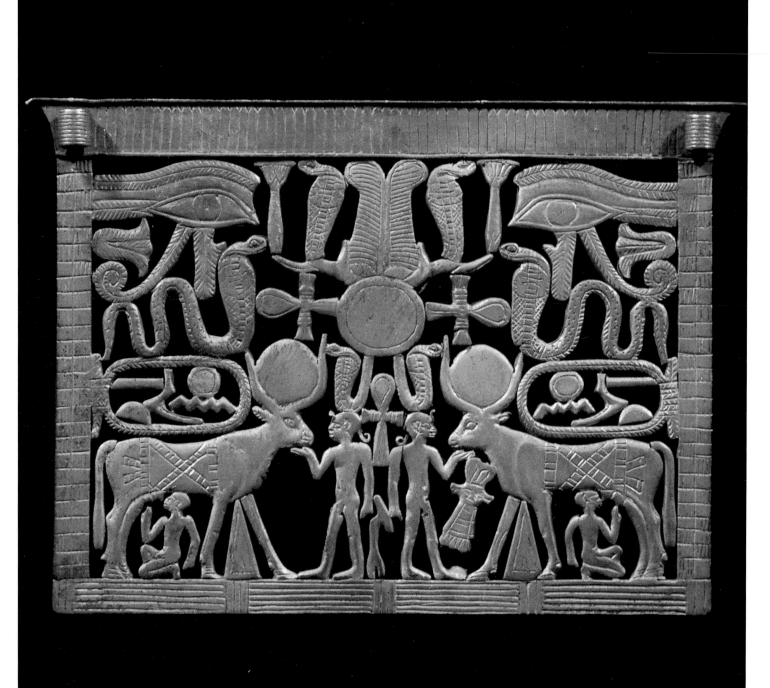

Although this find was soon overshadowed by the discovery of Tutankhamun's tomb only two years later, the ensemble of Middle Kingdom pieces was of a rare perfection and has been much admired by archaeologists. Never perhaps in the history of Egyptian jewelry had work of such quality, such harmony and such purity been achieved, either before or since. The refinement of this art bore witness to the high degree of civilisation of the Middle Kingdom, the classical period of pharaonic Egypt.

The pectoral: skill and symbol

Among the different kinds of jewelry produced by Egyptian goldsmiths, the pectoral (a type of pendant) occupies a special place. As we have already observed, during the Middle Kingdom, pectorals often imitated the form of the facade of a building, along the top of which ran a cavetto cornice. They thus resembled a small naos. On an openwork ground, polychrome motifs would be held in place by a golden frame. The back of the pectoral was generally carved, so that both sides of the object would be beautiful to behold – one embedded with precious stones, the other pure gold, so as better to display the skills of the craftsman.

The eminent expert on Egyptian jewelry, Emile Vernier, has made a detailed study of the cloisonné technique that is characteristic of these pectorals. He has shown how the Middle Kingdom craftsmen would prepare a piece of gold of the required shape, onto which they would solder narrow ridges. These ridges would serve as borders within which could be mounted carefully-calibrated stones and pieces of glass that had been cut to the precise dimensions required.

Both Jacques de Morgan and Emile Vernier have shown how the designs of these pectorals were closely related to the symbolism of monarchy and religion. They combine the ruling pharaoh's cartouche with figures that are emblematic of his power, such as the sovereign abusing negro and asiatic prisoners. In addition, there would be a protective sign – the image of the goddess Nekhbet, the falcon of the god Horus or griffons sporting the feathers of Amun on their heads.

The jewelry of the Middle Kingdom marks the high point of Egyptian goldwork. These objects, some four thousand years old, were doubtless much indebted to the work of the goldsmiths of the Old Kingdom. Unfortunately, too few examples have survived for us to form an accurate picture of the state of this craft in earlier times.

An unusual Egyptian diadem from Byblos

Montet discovered this beautiful gold repoussé work diadem in the tomb of the Phoenecian king Abi Shemu. The uraeus is in bronze inlaid with gold wire. No object of this kind has ever been found in Egypt. It may have been made expressly for the king of Byblos. It is decorated with motifs such as the djed pillar, the symbol of strength, and the key of life. (Beirut Museum, Lebanon.)

Opposite

A Middle Kingdom pectoral from the treasure of Byblos

The treasure of Byblos was discovered in 1924 by the French archaeologist Pierre Montet. Dating from the XXth and XIXth centuries BC, it includes a range of jewels of Egyptian origin. XIIth dynasty rulers maintained close trading relationships with the Phoenecian ports, from whence they imported cedarwood. This pectoral of the pharaoh Amenemhet III is decorated with several symbols intended to endow it with protective power: the wedjat eye and the uraeus are combined with the cult of the goddess Hathor, shown here as a cow holding the solar disk between her horns. (Beirut Museum, Lebanon.)

Jewelry and fashion during the Middle Kingdom

This painted limestone bas relief, portraying the royal concubine Achait, was found in the temple of Montjuhotep at Deir el Bahri (Thebes), excavated before the First World War by the Swiss Egyptologist Edouard Naville. The work dates from the XIth dynasty (c. 2000 BC) and shows the young woman wearing a large gorget over the straps of her dress. This necklace forms a plain surface on which are marked out a small chain, a string of cylindrical lapis lazuli beads and a garland of gold cowries, typical of Middle Kingdom art. The young Achait, a priestess of Hathor, is shown here savouring a sweet-scented blue lotus.
(Egyptian Museum, Cairo.)

Opposite

**A bracelet belonging
to Queen Ahhotep**

Queen Ahhotep's reign brought
the XVIIth dynasty to a close.
She was buried by Ahmose,
founder of the XVIIIth dynasty
(c. 1550 BC). Her coffin and
treasure were discovered
by Mariette in 1859 at Dra Abul
Naga (Thebes). Among her
jewels was this rigid gold
articulated bracelet. On a lapis
lazuli background, it depicts the
enthroned god Geb, representing
the earth. He is wearing
the crowns of Upper and Lower
Egypt, and is shown granting
his protection to the kneeling
king. Height: 3.4 cm (1³/₈ in).
(Egyptian Museum, Cairo.)

Following pages

**A necklace of Ahhotep
decorated with three gold flies**

This piece was found in the
queen's tomb. Three solid gold
flies hang from a chain.
The restrained treatment,
with schematic, yet highly
elegant forms, is typical
of early New Kingdom art.
Length of flies: 9 cm (3¹/₂ in).
(Egyptian Museum, Cairo.)

The treasure of Queen Ahhotep

Asiatic immigrants from Canaan first arrived in the Delta as
migrant workers in around 1750 BC. Taking courage from their
numbers and spurred on by invaders who had overrun their
homeland, they soon began to establish themselves as a military
force. They first seized power in Memphis, before going on to
build their own capital at Avaris.

The establishment of the Hyksos, as they were known to the
Egyptians, on the throne of the pharaohs of Lower Egypt marked
the end of the Middle Kingdom. In Upper Egypt, the Theban
kings resisted as best they could, until the pharaoh Sekenenrea,
and then his son Kamosis, reconquered Middle Egypt. The
Hyksos king Apophis sought to ally himself with the Nubians in
order to surround Thebes in a pincer movement, but in vain. In
around 1580, Ahmose, son of Kamosis, captured first Memphis,
then Avaris, and expelled the foreigners. He then went on to
found the glorious XVIIIth dynasty. His successor, Amenophis I,
completed the work of restoring order throughout the country,
and re-establishing its former power.

An empty coffin

Ahmose was buried at Dra Abul Naga, near Qurna, part of the
Theban necropolis. There he was worshipped alongside his mother,
Ahhotep, who had held the reins of power until the coming of age
of the young pharaoh. The incredible succession of events following the discovery of the funerary treasures of Queen Ahhotep in
January 1859 took place at around the time when archaeological
digs were first being formally organised in Egypt. Auguste Mariette
(1821-1881) had just founded the department of Antiquities and
the Egyptian Museum in Cairo, where he displayed the finds that
had been made in the Serapeum at Saqqara. He himself was
meanwhile pursuing his research in the field, on the west bank at
Thebes. It was there that he came upon the coffin of Queen
Ahhotep, which had been found intact at Dra Abol Naga.

Unfortunately, Mariette has left no formal record of his discovery. But we do know that this rich collection of jewelry survived
being pirated away only by a miracle. The coffin, en route to
Cairo Museum to be catalogued, was intercepted by the governor
of Qena who had got wind of the find. His first act was to open
the coffin and take all the jewelry, not hesitating to break into the
mummy, so as to remove the treasures it contained as swiftly as
possible.

Then, in the hope of winning the good favour of Saîd Pasha,
viceroy of Egypt and son of Mohammed Ali, the governor took

**Ahmose's dagger, found
in Queen Ahhotep's coffin**

The presence of weapons in a queen's grave
may strike us as surprising, but it was a natural
consequence of the final stages of the Egyptian
struggle against the Hyksos invaders. This piece
is a ceremonial arm that had belonged
to Ahmose. The gold-covered blade is
embellished with a central band of niello.
At the hilt, two holes pass between the horns
of a bull's head acting as a ferrule. The gold
pommel is decorated with reliefs of female heads,
while the sheath is made of two plain soldered
sheets of gold. Total length: 28.5 cm (11¼ in).
(Egyptian Museum, Cairo.)

Following pages

A ceremonial axe from the Queen's tomb

Among the treasures found piled up in Ahhotep's
coffin, was this large ceremonial gold axe
measuring 47.5 cm (18¾ in) long. The curved
cedarwood handle is covered with gold. Plaited
gold ribbons hold the copper blade in place.
The blade is decorated with gold, lapis lazuli,
enamel and niello.
The front of the blade bears the cartouches
of Ahmose, above the figure of the pharaoh
striking a Hyksos enemy, together with a griffon.
On the back, beneath the symbol of eternity,
are the emblems of Upper and Lower Egypt
(papyrus and lotus), as well as a reclining sphinx
in the effigy of the king holding a puzzle
in his hand. (Egyptian Museum, Cairo.)

the spoils of his pillage and set off by boat down the Nile to the
viceroy's palace in Cairo.

News of the theft, however, had reached Mariette. The
Frenchman was determined not to let himself be intimidated.
Hiring a steamship of his own, he set off in hot pursuit.
Eventually, Mariette caught up with the governor's boat and its
precious cargo. On boarding, he straightaway declared that he
was authorized by law to seize any goods which might contra-
vene the regulations governing the trade in antiquities. Although
the governor resisted, and it was necessary to resort to force,
Mariette managed to recover the treasure of Ahhotep and restore
it to its rightful owner: the Museum of the Egyptian nation, in
Cairo.

Fortunately, Saîd Pasha chose not to take offence and settled,
so the story goes, for a simple golden chain with a scarab beetle
pendant, as a present for his favourite mistress.

Reflections of troubled times

The Second Intermediate Period saw Egypt entering into political and artistic eclipse under the Hyksos. The quality of goldwork produced at this time inevitably suffered. The objects
found at Dra Abul Naga, whatever their beauty and their importance, were nowhere near as perfect as those which have survived
from the Middle Kingdom. The chaos which followed upon the
century-long occupation of a large part of the country can be
clearly seen in these pieces. It is evident both in a relative technical regression, and in the presence of ceremonial arms in the provisions buried alongside the dead queen. This apparent incon-
gruity provides a good idea of the troubles besetting Egypt at a
time when the people were fighting to reconquer their own land.

Thus among the "jewelry" of Ahhotep we can find not only
necklaces, bracelets and pectorals, but also a hatchet and a
dagger with its sheath. Almost all of these objects, including the
jewelry, are stamped with the cartouche of the pharaoh Ahmose,
even though they were found in the grave of his mother.

The hatchet, which has a copper blade and a cedarwood
handle, is entirely covered with gold. The blade is bound to
the handle with flat gold bands which serve a similar purpose to
the cord or leather thongs used to bind flints in the prehistoric
period. These bands form a criss-crossing pattern, like a tress.
Each side of the blade is worked with a different cloisonné pattern. On one side, three superimposed motifs combine the symbol
of eternity, the images of Upper and Lower Egypt, and, near to
the cutting edge, the king represented as a leonine sphinx. The
other side features the cartouches of the pharaoh Ahmose, the

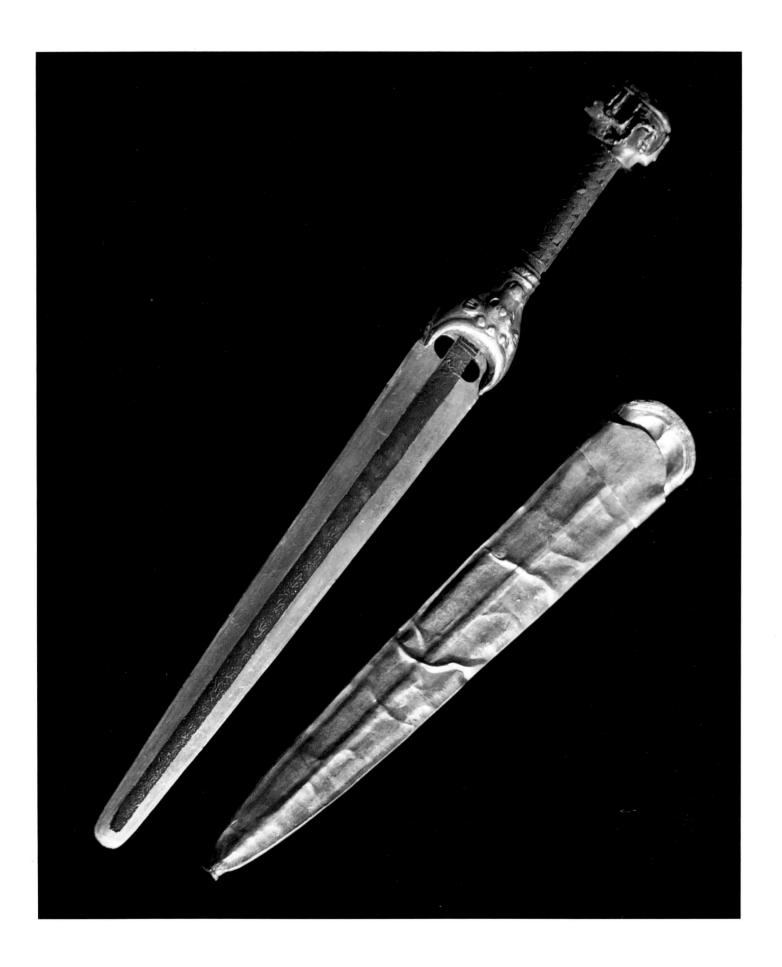

king striking a Hyksos prisoner whom he grasps by the hair, and a griffon.

On the curved handle, entirely covered with an openwork design in gold, appears an inscription of the royal protocol of Ahmose. The materials used in the cloisonné work are cornaline, lapis lazuli – generally blackened owing to decomposition – and a mock turquoise enamel.

Ahmose's dagger has a wooden handle covered in gold and decorated with triangles of cornaline, lapis lazuli and electrum. It terminates in a knob decorated with four reliefs of female heads. The hilt is formed out of a number of heads of Apis, whose horns surround the base of the openwork blade. The blade itself is covered with gold at the edges, and along the centre runs a niello rib. "Niello", according to Emile Vernier, "is a metallic sulphur which goldsmiths use as they would a black enamel". It is a mixture of silver, copper, lead, sulphur and sal ammoniac in fixed proportions. The resulting paste is calcined. On the dark background of the niello is an inscription in crimped gold wire.

The Queen's jewels

Among the jewels found in the coffin of Ahhotep are several bracelets made using quite different techniques. One is in solid gold, made of rigid segments, with two hinges. Around its circumference are scenes depicted in gold on a lapis lazuli background, and fixed in place using a kind of putty. These include two effigies of the god Geb, who personifies the earth, sitting back to back, each on his own throne. They protect the pharaoh, who is kneeling, and wears a uraeus on his head. The gods wear either the crown of Lower Egypt, or the double crown (the pschent). Gold cartouches identify the pharaoh as Ahmose. On the other side, there are four kneeling genies with the heads of jackals or sparrowhawks. Although the scene has an undeniable magnificence, the figures are squat and the design somewhat crude.

A rigid gold bracelet for the upper arm features the silhouette of a vulture with wings outspread. This is an extremely elegant piece; the feathers are treated in cloisonné work using lapis lazuli, cornaline and turquoise. Similarly, a group of flexible bracelets made out of gold beads, lapis, cornaline and turquoise strung on gold wire, simply reuse techniques already familiar under the Middle Kingdom. The decoration is formed out of repetitive motifs based on alternating triangles.

We should also mention a highly original chain from which three solid-gold flies are suspended with their wings outstretched. These figures are striking for their economical and restrained

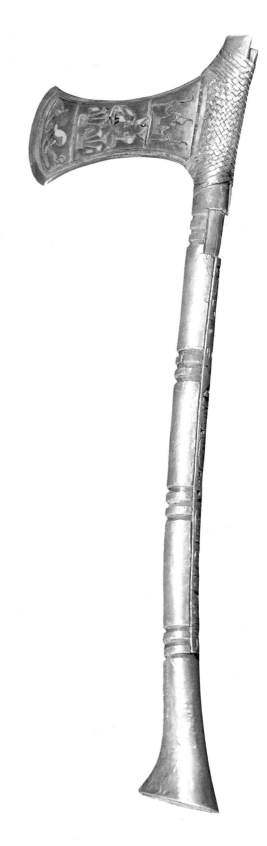

**Victorious pharaoh sacrificing
prisoners to Amun**

This drawing, made by Champollion in the rock
temple at Abu Simbel in Nubia, illustrates
the ritual use of weapons. Ramesses II is striking
negro and asiatic prisoners with his club in order
to propitiate the god Amun (on the left). Amun
is depicted wearing the twin plume and holding
a battle axe in his hand. This colourful
composition, published in 1835, reflects the
admirable state of preservation of the great speos
a mere century and a half ago. Today, all trace
of coloured painting has utterly vanished.

Following pages

Two jewels celebrating a rebirth

Left: rigid upper-arm bracelet in gold, decorated
with polychrome cloisonné feathers, representing
Nekhbet the vulture, goddess of the sky. From
the coffin of Queen Ahhotep. Height: 7.3 cm
(2⁷/₈ in). (Egyptian Museum, Cairo.)

Right: openwork pectoral in the form of a pylon,
depicting the ritual purification of the pharoah
Ahmose by the gods Ra-Horakhty and Amun
who hold baptismal ewers. This piece, from
Ahhotep's treasure, marks a revival
in the cot of goldwork in the early years
of the New Kingdom. Height: 7.2 cm (2⁷/₈ in).
(Egyptian Museum, Cairo.)

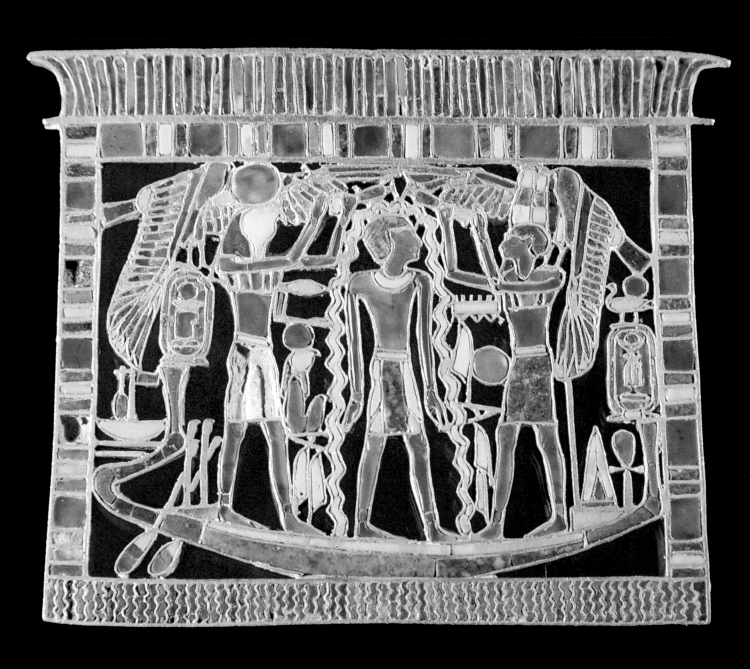

manner. Finally, there is a classic openwork pectoral, in the form of a temple pylon above which runs a cavetto cornice. The scene depicted is quite splendid. There are three figures in a boat: the central figure, the pharaoh Ahmose, is being purified with lustral water by the god Ra on the one side, with his falcon's head symbolising Lower Egypt, and, on the other, the god Amun, with two feathers rising above his head, symbolising Upper Egypt. Both gods are protected by royal falcons. Once again, the polychrome cloisonné has been produced using carefully graded stones.

The patera of General Djehuty

This splendid solid-gold patera was a present from Tuthmosis III to his skilful general Djehuty, who was his ambassador to the kings of Knossos. Made in around 1480 BC, it is testimony to the perfection achieved by the goldsmiths of the New Kingdom. Both the elegant Nile fish swimming beneath papyrus umbels and the superb hieroglyphs stamped around its edge demonstrate that the art of goldwork had already attained new heights.

Besides this exceptionally magnificent piece, the reign of Tuthmosis III has also bequeathed to us the contents of the tomb of the pharaoh's three widows. In 1916, after a period of torrential rain, a collection of jewels were found there by the ever-active unofficial excavators of the Qurna region. After some delicate negotiations, the American Herbert Winlock was able to acquire most of them for the Metropolitan Museum of Art in New York, where they were carefully restored.

These pieces illustrate the high standards that Egyptian goldwork had once again attained on the eve of the Amarna crisis which was soon to be sparked off by Amenophis IV, alias Akhenaten. They are one of a few rare collections to have survived from the powerful XVIIIth dynasty. As such, they help us to understand the high level of technical (if not artistic) achievement demonstrated by the treasure of the heretic pharaoh's successor, Tutankhamun.

Opposite

Goldwork and the insignia of power

Although many pharaonic jewels have survived down to the present day, one particular type, the highly ornate and symbolic crown, is familiar to us only from tomb paintings. This royal effigy, copied by Rosellini in around 1820 from a Theban tomb, depicts the impressive head-dress worn by the pharaoh on top of his nemes and uraeus. The rigid hat is decorated with eight solar cobras and sprouts the horns of Khnum, the creator deity, surmounted by a bouquet of flowers with two additional flanking cobras.

Below

Women in their finery

Another drawing by Rosellini, from the tomb of Nebomun, dating from the reign of Amenophis III. It depicts a group of seated musicians adorned with broad necklaces, bulky ear-rings, and many bracelets. Two of them are beating time, while a third plays on a double flute. They are presiding over a feast in celebration of the deceased.

A gold patera given by Tuthmosis III to his victorious general

Tuthmosis III, a warrior pharaoh of the XVIIIth dynasty, gave this beautiful
solid gold patera decorated with repoussé work (opposite, above) to general
Djehuty following the capture of the city of Haifa. The dish has a border
of papyrus bunches forming a garland beneath which swim six Nile fish
(detail above). The rim features a text with the royal cartouche, in
commemoration of the victory (opposite, below). The piece was found
at Dra Abul Naga, prior to the Tanis discoveries, and, at the time,
was one of the rare surviving examples of Egyptian goldware.
Diameter: 17 cm (6¾ in). (Musée du Louvre, Paris.)

Tomb of Sethos I: jewels of god and men

Tomb of Sethos I: jewels of god and men

The paintings in the tomb of Sethos I
(c. 1300 BC), the glorious XIXth dynasty pharaoh,
are amongst the finest in the Valley of the Kings
and illustrate the ritual function of jewelry
in ancient Egypt. This copy, made by Rosellini
in the burial chamber in around 1820, shows
the fair Hathor presenting a talisman-necklace
to the king (detail, pages 12-13). The two figures
are adorned with sumptuous jewelry including
gorgets, head-dresses, and both arm
and wrist bracelets (detail below).

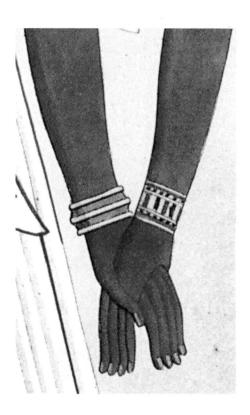

The reflected glory of the Ramessides

The most celebrated single period in the history of ancient Egypt is that of the Ramessides and the victorious warrior-pharaohs. It is also, in many art forms – architecture, sculpture, painting, everyday objects, and tombs, both grand and humble – the best known. The XIXth dynasty, which spans the reigns of Sethos I, Ramesses II and Sethos II (1310-1210 BC), is the richest century in Egyptian history for archaeological evidence, including the temples and the royal tombs of the Valley of the Kings, the tombs of ordinary citizens on the west bank at Thebes, as well as a wide variety of monuments scattered throughout the valley of the Nile, from Per-Ramesses in the Delta, to Abu Simbel in Upper Nubia.

It was a period of grandeur and abundance, thanks to the tribute paid by the peoples of Asia and Africa who had been brought under the sway of the pharaohs. This wealth was not an end in itself: it played an essential role in the process by which the king was transfigured into a god. Like dress and protocol or temple ritual, jewelry was an indispensable element in the rite of divinisation. It contributed to the essential function of the ceremony: to place the pharaoh far beyond the reach of ordinary mortals, in a world where the presence of the gods was made manifest. In the "dressing up" that was required by this operation, goldwork came to play a central role. Tomb paintings depict gods wearing the same jewelry as kings. In the Egyptian mind, ornamentation was thus intended to emphasise the resemblance between the wearer and the gods themselves.

A heritage laid waste

Given the role which gold and precious stones played in these customs, one might have expected the richest period in Egyptian history to have bequeathed to us the most fabulous jewels. In fact, however, little gold work has come down to us from the XIXth dynasty. In the light of what we know of the magnificence of Egyptian life at that time, the little that remains of it today is quite startling. None of the great Theban tombs of the Ramessides has managed to keep its treasure intact down to the present day. In fact, all of it was stolen during a period of instability which began around 1100 BC, and which was to lead to the partition of Egypt during the Third Intermediate Period.

Throughout this time of revolt and social upheaval, pillaging the tombs of the kings and of the Theban aristocracy became a sort of local industry. Despite the heavy penalties inflicted on grave-robbers and those who violated sarcophagi, for many the

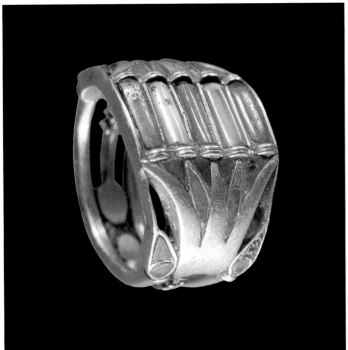

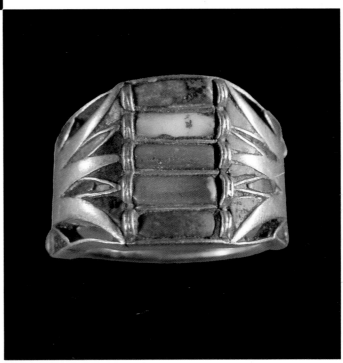

Opposite

A Ramesside liturgical vase

Another example of New Kingdom ritual ware.
This small gold vase was found in 1907 at Tell
Basta, formerly Bubastis, in the Delta. The tall
neck is decorated with recurrent rows of lotus
and small flower motifs while the belly is covered
with a pattern of starkly aligned seeds. The vase
features a ring, by which it could be hung.
This ring is slotted into a clasp in the form of
a reclining bull. Height: 11.2 cm (4⅜ in).
(Egyptian Museum, Cairo.)

Rings of the great Ramessides

The treasure of the most famous pharaohs
of Egypt is restricted to a few jewels, amongst
which are a series of rings made using different
techniques. Upper left and lower right, a lotus
cloisonné work ring made from lapis lazuli and
turquoise. The flat side is made from five
cylindrical stones mounted in parallel.
The two other rings – featuring horses (belonging
to Ramesses II) and ducks (Ramesses III) –
are more restrained in their use of anecdotal
imagery. (Musée du Louvre, Paris.)

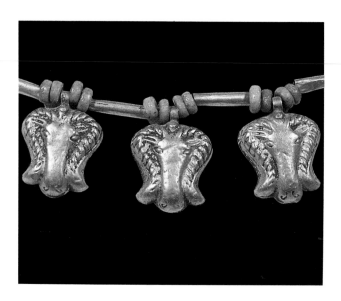

Chain with pendants representing Khnum, the goat

This XIXth dynasty piece stems from a long tradition of necklaces made up of gold relief amulets. The pendants were worked by beating out or blistering, both extremely ancient procedures. These techniques involve the use of a convex or concave form against which the gold leaf is hammered, allowing several identical objects to be produced. This necklace alternates the head of the god Khnum, creator of the world, and glass beads.
(Museo Egizio, Turin.)

Opposite

A period of great splendour

During the reign of Merenptah, the thirteenth son and immediate successor of Ramesses II (c. 1200 BC), Egypt was still basking under the glorious achievements of the "victor of Kadesh", who had stemmed the advancing Hittite armies. Merenptah's tomb is perhaps the most magnificent in the Valley of the Kings, as can be seen in this detailed drawing made by Rosellini in the early XIXth century. Besides the ceremonial sceptres and head-dresses, both the god Horus and the pharaoh are shown wearing the magnificent polychrome gorgets of which the Egyptians were so fond.

temptation was just too strong. Every hypogeum still intact was known to be piled high with gold and jewelry. Specialists soon appeared, genuine professionals of organised crime, who ran their teams like commando units, ready to swoop at the slightest sign of inattention on the part of the guards in the Valley of the Kings or Queens. At one point, the Prince of the West, who was in command of the soldiers detailed to the necropolis, even arranged with the royal inspectors to turn a blind eye to the thefts that plagued them. The bribes they shared under this arrangement were quite astronomical.

Sometimes, however, the crime could not be covered up. The guilty parties were hauled before the courts; across the gulf of three millennia, the minutes recorded on papyrus enable us to follow the proceedings. Howard Carter, who knew more than anyone else about the fate of each individual tomb in the Valley of the Kings, studied these sources during his search for the tomb of Tutankhamun. He quotes from verbatim reports of the thieves' own confessions: "After having opened the coffins, the accused confessed, we undid the shrouds, revealing the mummy of the famous king. Around his neck were many amulets and gold jewels, and around his head, a veritable sheet of gold. The body was decorated with a great quantity of precious stones. We seized the jewels and the talismans of the divine king, then made off with the sacred vessels: vases of gold, silver and bronze".

These raids assumed such proportions that the high priests of Amun began to look for a remedy. Secretly they decided to move, one by one, the mummies of the greatest pharaohs who had been buried in the Valley of the Kings since Tuthmosis I, in the hope of fooling the thieves. Yet the location of the mummies had to be repeatedly changed. Then Pinudjem, the high priest of Thebes around 1050 BC, thought to put to a stop to grave-robbing once and for all, by assembling the principal mummies of the great kings in a single spot, away from the official burial area. He installed forty of them in a hiding place in the cliff at Deir el Bahri. And there they lay, side by side in a crevice in the rock, for almost three thousand years.

However, all good things must come to an end. Some time around 1875, the most cunning of all Egyptian thieves came upon the hiding place of the glorious pharaohs. The clan of Abd el Rasul lived with their wives and children at Qurna, where they had occupied the finest Theban tombs. It was impossible to evict them. Abd el Rasul himself lived the life of a man of independent wealth. Every time he ran out of money, he would sell some piece of treasure that he had come across during his explorations that led him into every nook and cranny of the Theban mountainside. When a series of objects of outstanding quality suddenly appeared

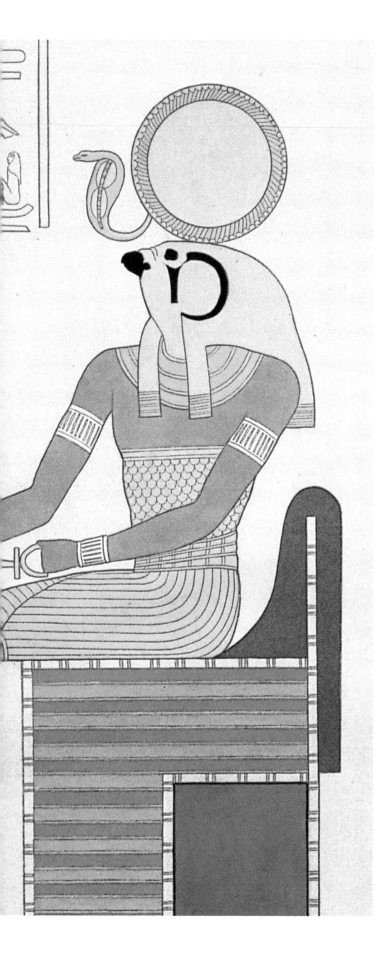

on the market for antiquities, the Egyptian Museum soon got wind of it. Maspéro, who was director at that time, reacted immediately, dispatching one of his assistants to find out where the objects had come from. Finally, an informer was found who was prepared to give the game away. Thus, in 1881, the archaeologist Emile Brugsch, guided by Abd el Rasul himself, entered the famous hiding place at Deir el Bhari and beheld the great mummies laid out there, amongst them Ramesses II, as well as Sethos I, Ahmose, Amenophis I and Tuthmosis III.

Too little time?

These mummies were certainly an important find, and they were shipped to the museum in Cairo. However, for the amateur of Egyptian gold work, the discovery was disappointing. There were no great treasures stowed away with them, since most of their riches had been stolen in ancient times. This explains why, today, we possess such scant evidence of the state of the goldsmith's art at the zenith of Egypt's imperial power.

Pillage alone, however, cannot explain everything. Fine gold bracelets decorated with stones set among granules, and pretty rings in cloisonné work or depicting tiny horses, have survived from the time of Ramesses II. But a pair of earrings bearing the name of Queen Tausret, the wife of Sethos I, are distinctly disappointing. Even the ceremonial gold vase unearthed at Bubastis, though charmingly decorated, is at best rustic in its technique, compared with work from the time of Tutankhamun. Nor does it bear comparison with later gold work from the period of Psusennes I, who reigned during the Third Intermediate Period, one of those phases of decline in Egyptian history whose artistic productions are all too often denigrated by the specialists.

Waves of gold

The violation of the pharaonic graves was not a continuous process, but came and went according to the vicissitudes of Egyptian history. When centralised power was strong, the king was able to ensure that the tombs of his predecessors were respected. When his authority was challenged, however, and the unity of the state was sapped by popular revolt, foreign invasion or feudal disaffection, the nomes (provinces) would reassert their independence, and the result was often rampant disorder. Whoever the thieves might be – invaders, local chiefs or ordinary people, desperate and hungry – pillage was always symptomatic of a return to anarchy.

In such circumstances, even the peace of the dead, so sacred to the Egyptians, was no longer respected. The treasures hidden

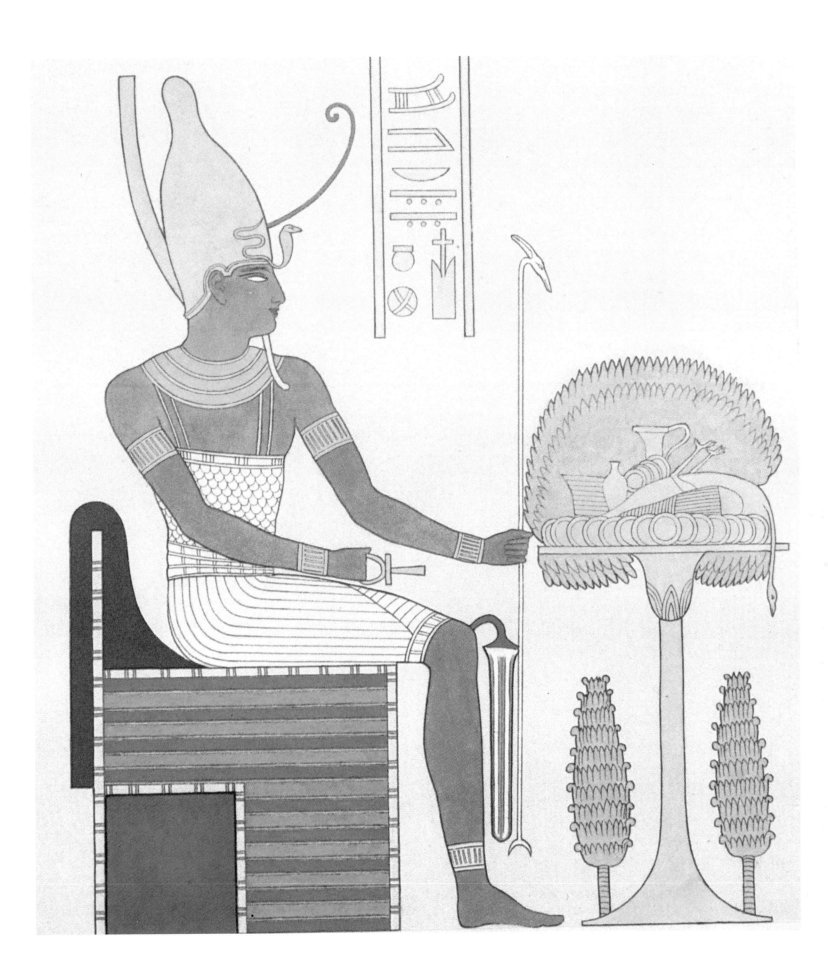

in their tombs proved too great a temptation, and operations to despoil them were organized on a grand scale. Bandits, working together in gangs, would ravage the necropolises, plundering tombs, ripping open chapels, removing burial provisions from mastabas and leaving behind them fields strewn with the ruins of once proud monuments.

Nothing was spared their depredations. Banditry became an exercise in "reappropriation" on an industrial scale. It served to redistribute wealth that had too long been concentrated in the hands of a minority. One by one, the tombs were opened and forced to yield up their treasures. Hypogea hollowed out of the rock were stripped of their riches by the poor who would break into the innermost sanctum of the pyramids to re-emerge, laden down with strange and magnificent objects.

The great necropolises, once dedicated to silence, now rang with the sound of battering rams and serpentine sledgehammers slamming against sealed doors, of crowbars and levers forcing their way under granite lids, of rubble tumbling down open shafts in underground galleries.

Sarcophagi were broken open, golden coffins were emptied of their mummies, sawn up and carried away piece by piece, masks of precious metal were torn from the faces of the dead and protective jewelry snatched from under hastily shredded bandages. What remained of the poor god-kings would then be ditched among the desert sands on the rocky screes of the mountains.

Such apocalyptic scenes were described in ancient texts, and occurred at several points in Egypt's history: at the end of the Old Kingdom, in around 2200 BC; during the Hyksos invasions in around 1750 BC; and again at the end of the New Kingdom, under Ramesses IX and his successors, from 1100 BC onwards.

Thus, while gold was never in widespread circulation as a form of money in ancient Egypt, being reserved for the religious and ornamental uses of an elite, it was continuously being "recycled". Each time the country entered a phase of decline, enormous masses of gold and silver were exhumed from the tombs of the kings, to be put to more mundane, and perhaps more urgent, uses.

In this way, tons of gold would periodically reappear on the market and find their way back into the goldsmiths' workshops. Together with the tribute paid by the Nubians, the Ethiopians and the subject peoples of the East, it would then be moulded into a different form and returned to the tombs from whence it came, to await discovery by a subsequent generation of treasure hunters.

Gold was already an object of fascination in Egypt four thousand years ago, at the time of the great revolution in civilisation.

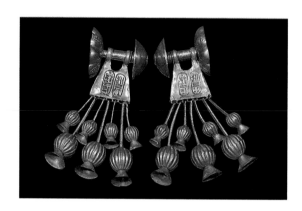

Queen Tausret's ear-rings

The art of the goldsmith began to decline well
before the end of the XXth dynasty. These gold
earrings, found in 1908, date from a period
of dynastic upheaval and are stamped with
the cartouche of Sethos II. The gross, ungainly
treatment is indicative of a regression
in metalworking technique. It has been claimed
that they may have been child's ear-rings
– an unlikely hypothesis given their actual size.
Length: 13.5 cm (5¼ in).
(Egyptian Museum, Cairo.)

Opposite

Ramesses IX in ceremonial dress

This drawing by Rosellini reveals how, under
the later Ramessides, ornamentation tended
to the extravagant. Gorgets had never been
so massive, nor gold ritual aprons so sumptuous.
Crowns and bracelets also were increasingly
impressive. The pharaoh is shown here offering
up an emblem of Maat, goddess of truth.

Following pages

**The great Ramesses portrayed
as military leader in his war chariot**

Drawn by galloping steeds, the pharaoh's proud
chariot hurtles down on the foe. This painted
relief from the speos at Abu Simbel was copied
by Champollion and shows that the king wore
his jeweled apparel into battle. Necklaces
and bracelets, including the broad protectivre
wristband worn by archers on their left arm,
were studded with precious stones and enamel.

Right up to Roman times, it never lost its power of attraction,
throughout the various periods of upheaval with which the country was afflicted. The first Christians violated tombs both to de-
stroy the pagan images within, and in order to get their hands on
their treasures. During the Middle Ages, sultans and caliphs
would organize full-scale expeditions, in order to replenish the
coffers of the state.

In modern times, two kinds of treasure hunter have competed
for what remained of the wealth of ancient Egypt: archaeologists,
who have sought to protect the information contained in these
magnificent objects by placing them in museums; and profes-
sional thieves, who lived among the ruins and the cemeteries,
which they scoured for objects they could then sell on to the
highest bidder. Among the thieves, the best known perhaps was
the head of the Abd el Rasul clan. He and his family and followers
lived on the inexhaustible site of Qurna, opposite Thebes, where
for centuries the fellahin had trafficked in illicit treasures.

Nowadays, treasure hunters are no longer motivated merely
by the intrinsic value of the metal an object contains. The extraordinary inflation of prices for antiquities on the art market has
made such trafficking even more irresistible, whatever the penalties for those unlucky enough to be caught. Thus, the gold of the
pharaohs continues to lure adventurers and criminals. Like lost
shards of the sun, it still shines in the darkness of the tombs,
filling the hearts of men with its fiery glow, its unquenchable
desire. Where Egypt's rulers saw the flesh of the gods, their successors see an easily accessible form of capital, and continue to
empty out the tombs in order to fill their bank accounts.

TANIS REVISITED

This lapis lazuli heart with a gold-plated clapper ring was discovered with Psusennes I in his tomb. It is engraved with images of the sun god. Height: 4.7 cm (1⅞ in). (Egyptian Museum, Cairo.)

In the spring of 1939, war in Europe was inevitable. For more than twelve years, Pierre Montet had been exploring an isolated site in the Nile Delta whose only surviving monuments had long been reduced to formless ruins. Montet was a French archaeologist, who had already made his reputation with the discovery of the magnificent graves, dating from 2000 BC, of the rulers of Byblos on the Phonecian coast (present-day Lebanon). Since 1928, he had been excavating at Tanis, in the wet lands lying between the many branches of the Nile where it flows into the Mediterranean. He was driven by the conviction that Lower Egypt, like the area around Thebes, must still contain many undiscovered marvels.

Rumours of war grew with news of the Anschluss and the Nazi threat loomed larger with every passing day. Munich had

Opposite

Bustling activity on the Tanis excavation-site in 1939

In the Delta, the former location of the city of Tanis – capital of the kingdom during the XXIst and XXIInd dynasties (1060-773 BC) – was signalled by a massive tumulus. From 1929 onwards, Pierre Montet conducted excavations here with the help of dozens of workers. Between 1939 and 1946, he brought to light the treasures of many lesser-known pharaohs.

demonstrated the Allies' incapacity to stand up to Hitler. Yet despite the imminent risk of crisis, the French mission continued to work on indefatigably.

The dig must go on

On 18 March 1939, Montet entered a tomb close to that of the pharaoh Osorkon, which he had discovered three weeks earlier. Osorkon's tomb had long been sacked. But as soon as Montet stepped into the newly opened vault, he realised that he must be the first person to have done so for three thousand years. Standing in the entrance to the vestibule, he could make out a silver sarcophagus with a falcon's head: "There was a gap, and through it I could see the gleam of gold within". Moreover, despite its small dimensions, the chamber was packed full of precious relics, and the floor was strewn with objects of every sort: figurines, canopic vases, bronze accessories, to mention but a few.

Then came the biggest surprise of all. Montet had read on the walls of the chamber a hieroglyphic inscription in the name of Psusennes I. "So we were in the tomb of Psusennes, the greatest of the pharaohs of Tanis". The silver sarcophagus, however, bore the cartouche of an unknown king, by the name of Hega Kheper-Ra Senonchis, no doubt a descendant or successor of the Senonchis whose name was familiar to readers of the Bible, for the Book of Kings mentions a pharaoh known as Senonchis who had sacked the Temple of Solomon in Jerusalem in 925 BC.

Unsuspected treasures

Although, due to the humidity of the low-lying land of the Delta, the mummy interred inside this enigmatic sarcophagus had entirely disintegrated, the golden jewelry he had worn had survived – necklaces, bracelets, amulets and an admirable golden mask. This Senonchis, the second to bear that name, reigned during a period of co-regency that had begun in around 890 BC, during the XXIInd dynasty. He belonged to that obscure period known to specialists as the Third Intermediate Period.

Despite its considerable importance, the discovery passed almost unnoticed. Europe had other preoccupations. Two days before Montet entered the tomb of Senonchis, the German army had invaded Czechoslovakia and captured Prague. In Spain, the fascist legions were bombarding the Republican forces. In such a context, even a discovery as sensational as that at Tanis merited no more than a few lines in the daily press. Most newspapers did, however, report that on 21 March 1939 the sarcophagus of an unknown king had been opened in the Nile Delta.

As every year, the dig was brought to a temporary halt at the end of April because of the heat. It was agreed, albeit with little conviction, that work would resume the following year. Mussolini had occupied Albania, and the armies of the Reich were preparing to invade Poland following the signing of the Germano-Soviet pact on 23 August. They crossed the border on 1 September and swept across through the Polish plains. The Allies, who had signed a mutual assistance pact, declared war on Hitler on 3 September 1939. Less than one month later, Warsaw fell to the Germans.

The tomb of Psusennes

By January 1940, Montet had resumed his excavations at Tanis, despite the international catastrophe that was unfolding in Europe. His team discovered the jewelry of Prince Hornakht in the grave of Osorkon II. Then, on 15 February, they stumbled on the door to a previously unentered vault, leading off the tomb of Psusennes. This chamber was opened on 21 February 1940, in the presence of King Farouk. So far, the phoney war had failed to hinder the exploration of the site. The archeologists now found themselves confronted by a walled-up door, which had been hidden behind paintings of ritual scenes. An enormous block of granite had to be eased out of place; through the gaps to each side they could see the glimmering of metal objects.

Once the obstacle had been removed, an impressive pink granite sarcophagus was revealed. Around about, hundreds of objects and shabtis lay strewn across the floor. A number of pieces immediately stood out amidst the clutter: a fine silver table for offerings, a bronze stove, three solid gold vases, and several finely-worked gold goblets and chalices.

The granite sarcophagus was intact. It had originally belonged to Merenptah, then had been reused for the burial of Psusennes. The magnificent sculpted lid was opened with great pomp. Inside lay a second black granite sarcophagus, which was opened some days later on 28 February, revealing yet a third dusty grey metal container that had been extensively worked and chased. This was the silver coffin of Psusennes I of the XXIst dynasty. The lid bore the features of the king who had ruled at Tanis from 1036 to 989 BC. The assembled archeologists were left speechless by the sheer beauty of the piece with its gold embellishment.

An extraordinary catalogue

The final sarcophagus was opened on 1 March. The occasion was a dramatic one. The bottom of the silver box had been corroded by water (omnipresent at Tanis) and broke; only the lid

A majestic image

In this gold mask, Psusennes I is depicted wearing the nemes and uraeus, a false beard and a broad, many-stranded gorget. Only the eyes, eyebrows and beard are highlighted in enamel. The piece was worked by swageing, and the back of the head is composed of a thick sheet of gold leaf riveted to the front. The repoussé work has been executed with a chasing-tool. The beaten gold still bears traces of the hammering-out process, and this confers a certain vibrancy to the royal effigy, almost seeming to bring it back to life.
Height: 48 cm (18⅞ in).

Opposite

A mask comparable to that of Tutankhamun

The greatest surprise in store for Montet and his team came on 23 February 1940, when they opened the silver coffin. Inside, they discovered the extraordinary death mask of Psusennes I. How, they mused, could the remains of such an obscure pharoah have been buried in such splendour? (Egyptian Museum, Cairo.)

Psusennes' funerary jewels

Dressing the mummy in gold formed part of the burial ritual. Provided with a death mask, he was placed under a large "overcoat" – a sheet of chased gold one metre (39 in) long, enveloping him from chest to ankles. His hands were adorned with gold fingerstalls, decorated with rings, and the toes of his feet were treated in similar fashion (opposite, above). He was also shod with magnificent gold sandals of a design dating back to prehistoric models, hence their restrained elegance (opposite, below). Length: 23.5 cm (9¼ in).
(Egyptian Museum, Cairo.)

could be lifted out. Those present were first struck by surprise then filled with admiration at the purity of design of the king's gold mask and the splendour of his jewelry. The pitiful remains of the body were hidden beneath a "blanket" of chased gold, along with thirty rings, twenty-two bracelets, fingerstalls and sandals of gold, and many other splendid jewels, including pectorals, scarabs, necklaces and talismans. All that was left of the mummy, however, were a few bones.

Meanwhile, Russian troops were fighting the Finns and German submarines patrolled the Atlantic, preying on Allied convoys. The fantastic discoveries at Tanis passed almost unnoticed amidst the clamour of war. Yet Montet and his team continued their explorations, undeterred. On 16 April, they discovered the tomb of Amenemipet, an unknown pharaoh whose jewelry, though less abundant than that of Psusennes, "was nevertheless most fine".

Owing to the international situation, it became urgent to pack the treasure discovered at Tanis in crates and transfer it to the Museum in Cairo, where it arrived on 3 May. May 1940 ushered in France's darkest hour of the entire war, as the Belgian and

144

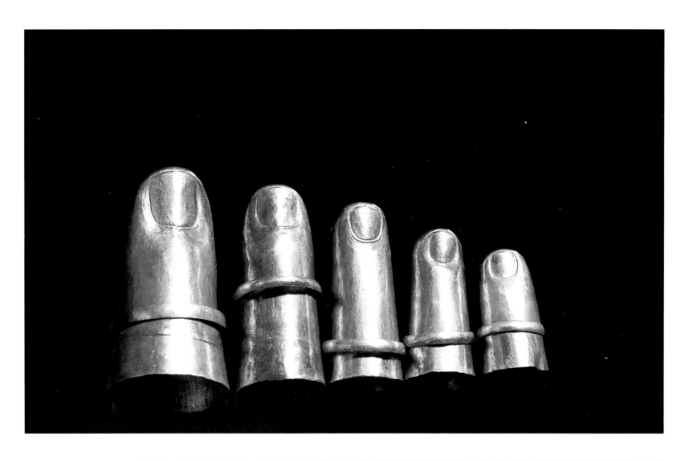

Omnipresent gold, bestowing eternal life on the deceased

In addition to the fine gold mask, the idealised features of which are the outcome of much patient swageing, the body of the pharaoh was also dressed with gold jewels and clothes. The sheet of gold repoussé work shown on the right, for instance, was used to mask the incision made by the embalmers to remove the entrails of the dead king. This "truss" is decorated with the protective wedjat eye, surrounded by the four spirits who guard the canopic vases. Width: 16.6 cm (6½ in). (Egyptian Museum, Cairo.)

Dutch frontiers crumbled before the onslaught of the *Panzerdivisionen*. By 31 May, the Allied débâcle had reached its nadir at Dunkirk. On 14 June, the German army entered Paris. Three days later, Marshal Pétain sued for peace. On 18 June, an unknown General by the name of Charles de Gaulle called on all free French forces to rally to him in London.

1945: excavations resume

Depite his certainty that there were still many other tombs to be explored at Tanis, Montet had to wait another five years before resuming his search. The fate of his country kept him away from Egypt until April 1945. By then, France had been liberated, though the war was not yet over. The final Russian

offensive against Berlin began on 17 April. By the time the fighting had drawn to a close in Europe on 8 May 1945, work had already begun again at Tanis.

A further campaign of excavations proved necessary, in the course of which the team discovered the tomb of Wendjebaundjed, a general of the pharoah's archers and royal favourite, who had been laid to rest not far from his master. Prospections carried out by Alexandre Lézine, an architect who worked with Montet, enabled them to locate this small tomb right beside the main chamber.

The tomb was opened on 13 February 1946. Wendjebaundjed lay surrounded by the most magnificent objects, jewels and offerings: paterai, cups of gold and silver, beautiful pectorals, massive pendants in the shape of Bastet the cat or the goddess Isis, and

Following pages

The insignia of power

Several emblems of power were found in the tomb of Psusennes I, including a rod and a sword. The rod is made from a tube of gold and bears inscriptions with the royal cartouche, together with a round pommel. The sword, its blade entirely rusted away, was found in the pink granite sarcophagus. The gold-plated handle is in the form of the falcon Horus. The bird's head is represented with great delicacy, and the body is covered with subtle decorative plumage. (Egyptian Museum, Cairo.)

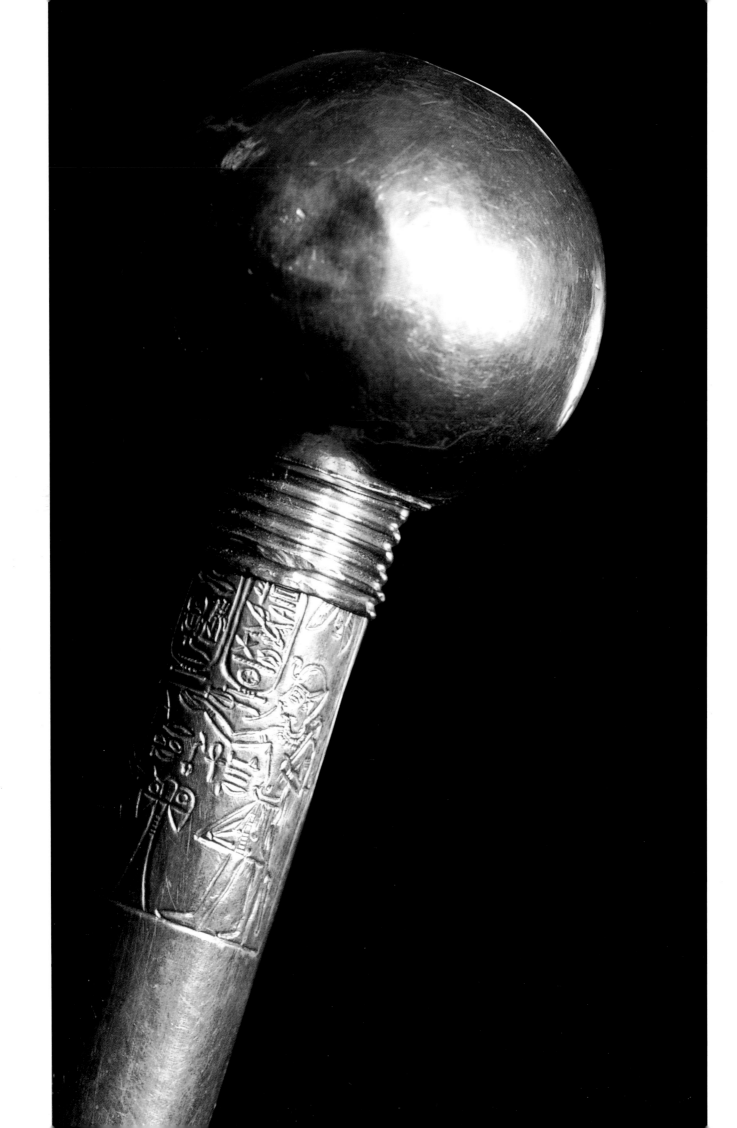

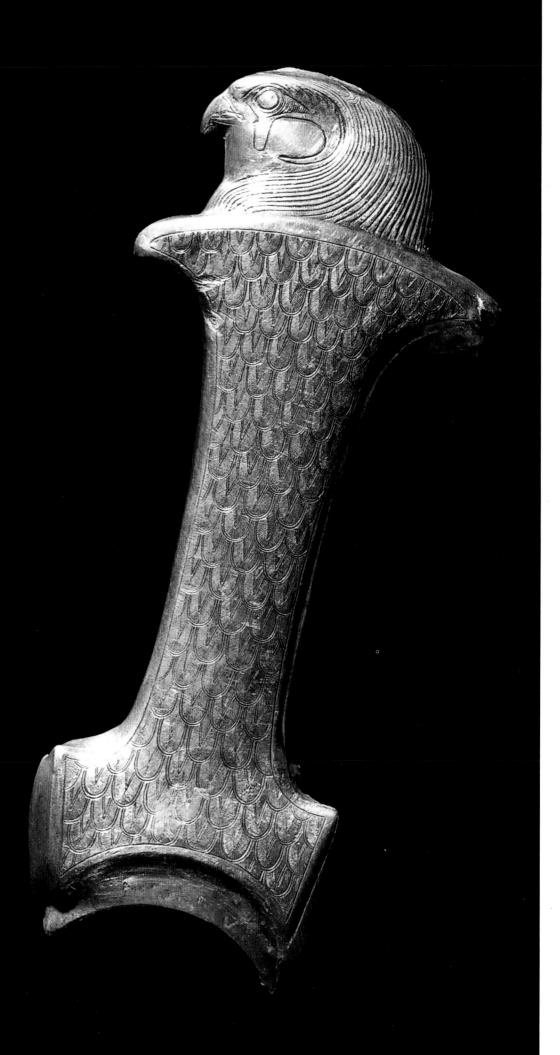

The jewelry of Psusennes I

When they opened the sarcophagus of Psusennes to discover the silver coffin decorated with gold details, Montet and his team realised that they were dealing with a period in Egyptian history when silver, once a commodity even rarer than gold, must have been in plentiful supply, a fact that indicated close trading relations with Near Eastern Asia. The flow of silver from Syria to Egypt proved that the pharaohs had not been cut off from all their Asiatic sources. Although Tanis in the Delta may only have had indirect access to the gold mines in the south, controlled by the priest-kings of Thebes, the sovereigns of Lower Egypt were evidently in a position to commission the making of solid silver coffins.

The earliest Egyptian myths describe the gods as possessing silver bones, golden flesh and lapis lazuli beards. Gold was therefore still an important part of the burial rite. The Tanite pharaohs used gold only for the king's effigy and for the most important items of apparel in which he would be dressed after mummification. Chief among these was the traditional death mask, which was his face in the afterworld. Psusennes' mask was very similar to that of Tutankhamun, save for the details in precious stones and enamel. Also crucial was the "overcoat" of chased gold which covered the mummy. Underneath this covering, the mummy wore gold fingerstalls on both hands and feet, a gold disembowling plate to conceal the scar left by the embalming process, chased gold sandals and a gold-handled sword. Gold talismans were sewn onto his shroud, and a lapis lazuli heart with a clapper ring, used in the ritual of psychostasis, was also present. These specific elements made up the mummy's ornamentation and apparel. There were also liturgical vessels and the pharaoh's amulets, often remarkably ornate for such a relatively inglorious period.

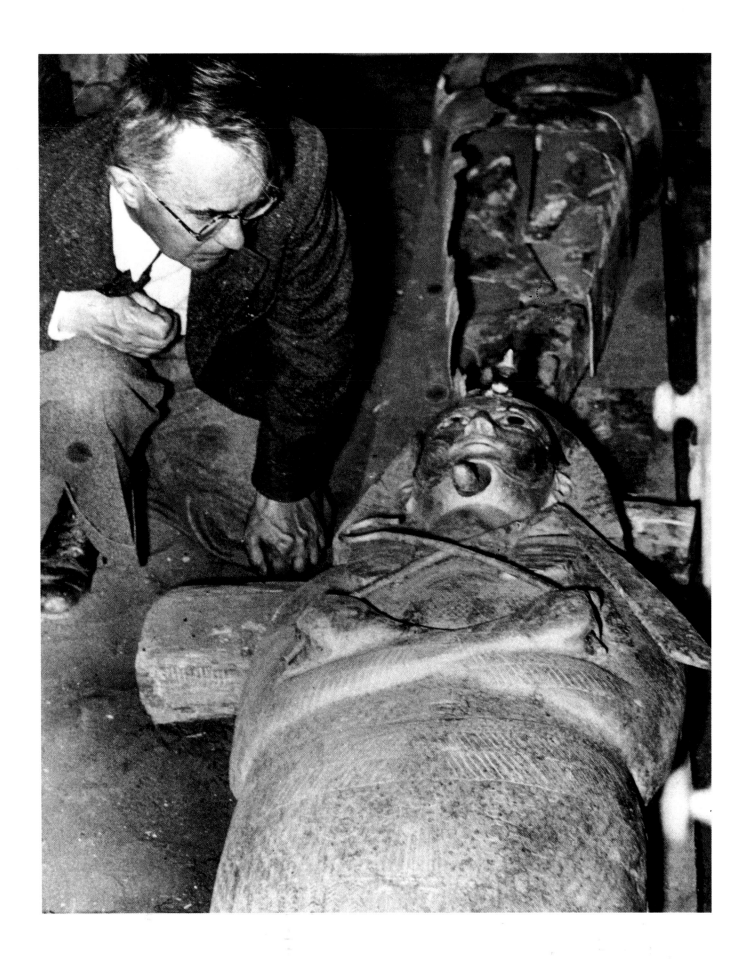

several bracelets given him by Psusennes himself. There were also pieces the Head Archer had inherited from Ramesses II.

This discovery brought to a close a sensational series of finds that the war and its aftermath had managed to obscure more or less completely from European eyes. The treasure of Tanis should now be recognized for what it is: one of the most important collections of goldwork to have come down to us from pharaonic times, and one which in many respects bears comparison with the treasure of Tutankhamun.

Who was Pierre Montet?

The man responsible for these extraordinary and, still to this day, underrated discoveries, was born in the Beaujolais region of France on 27 June 1885. By the time he struck lucky in Egypt, he was already fifty-four. This, however, was by no means the first feather in his cap, as can be seen by a brief consideration of his earlier career.

Pierre Montet began to study Egyptology in 1905. In 1910, he was working at the French Institute for Eastern Archaeology in Cairo, as a member of the team excavating the site of Abu Rosh near Giza. Later, he worked in Middle Egypt, on the four-thousand-year-old tombs to be found at Asyut and Beni Hasan.

From there, he set out on an expedition to the desert mountains of Wadi Hammamat in Upper Egypt, the site of one of the oldest gold mines between the Nile and the Red Sea. On his return, Montet published a series of inscriptions that he had discovered in this wild and arid landscape.

He was conscripted during the First World War, and carried out missions in the Near East, in particular to Syria. In 1919, once the war was over, he was appointed to teach Egyptology at the University of Strasbourg. At the same time, he was in charge of the research being carried out in Phoenecia into the history of the ancient city of Gebal, also known as Byblos, following the prospections made by Ernest Renan at the end of the previous century. He discovered the tombs of the Kings of Byblos, with whom the Pharaohs of Egypt had been in close contact from the Old Kingdom onwards (c. 2700 BC). Egypt had relied on the coast of Lebanon for supplies of cedar wood. Thus, among the funerary trappings at Gebal, Montet found many Egyptian jewels that had been presents from the rulers of the Middle Kingdom.

Inspired by his reading of the Bible, Montet scoured the shores of Palestine for traces of the peoples who had had dealings with Ancient Egypt. In 1928 he published a book under the title *Byblos and Egypt*, detailing his discoveries. At the same time, determined to uncover evidence of the presence of the Hebrew

What did the sarcophagus of Psusennes I contain?

The crucial moment: Montet and an Egyptian assistant prepare to open the pink granite sarcophagus on 21 February 1940.
This photograph, taken during the "phoney war", suggests something of the archaeologists' impatience.

Opposite

Pierre Montet examining the silver coffin of Psusennes

Crouched beside his extraordinary discovery, Montet is inspecting the state of preservation of the metal. In the background can be seen the silver base of the coffin which disintegrated when the team attempted to extract it.

nation on Egyptian soil, he decided to undertake explorations in the Delta. He chose the site of Tanis, at that time still little known. Indeed, it was often confused with the city of Per-Ramesses (the fortified royal palace that had been built to stem the advance of the Hittites across the Near East), and with Avaris, which had been the capital of the Hyksos invaders during the late Middle Kingdom (1750-1600 BC).

Montet knew that the humid climate of the Delta, unlike the arid heat of Upper Egypt, made it far less likely that any organic remains would have been preserved. But he still hoped to find stone and metal objects, and in this respect, his intuitions were to be proved right. Yet the dig that he began in 1928 only bore fruit in 1939. For over ten years, Montet's patience was sorely tested, as Carter's had been right up to the moment when he found the tomb of Tutankhamun.

When, finally, Montet did discover a perfectly preserved tomb at Tanis, his enthusiasm, and that of those around him, knew no bounds. Unfortunately, the virtually simultaneous outbreak of the Second World War meant they had little time to proceed with due scientific caution. Montet found himself reluctantly trapped in a race against the clock. The meticulous procedures a find of this importance deserved were out of the question. The rumour of an outstanding discovery spread like wildfire in Lower Egypt. In such troubled times, these objects could not be left where they had been found without swiftly falling prey to thieves.

And thus, the glorious discovery turned into a "salvage" operation, similar to those carried out many years later in Nubia, when monuments and treasures had to be hurriedly saved from the rising waters of the Nile during the construction of the Aswan high dam. Yet, even if there are too few photographs, and the scientific records are hastily or inadequately compiled, Montet managed to pull the job off with great skill, despite the pressure he was under. The book he published on the find is a superb piece of scholarship, far more impressive than many that have been produced by archaeologists who had all the time in the world. Entitled *The Royal Necropolis of Tanis*, it appeared in three substantial volumes between 1947 and 1960, and describes every single object found on the site.

The major discoveries made at Tanis between 1939 and 1946 may not have made Montet a public celebrity, but they did bring him the highest honours the scientific community can bestow. He was called to teach at the Collège de France, and elected to the Académie des Inscriptions et Belles-Lettres, of which he became President in 1963. He was also President of the Institut de France. He continued to work with the same energy and enthusiasm right up to his death in 1966 at the age of eighty-two.

A period of decline?

The discoveries Montet made at Tanis are astonishing in more than one respect. First of all, they shed light on the art of what had previously been a highly obscure period in Egyptian history. From the treasures found there, it is now obvious that the metal-work of that period was far from mediocre. On the contrary, a majority of the pieces Montet found display skilled workmanship of the highest order.

However, these finds also prove that the eclipse postulated by scholars when they baptized this period the "Third Intermediate Period" was far from being the dramatic decline previously imagined.

Admittedly, there was no unified authority during the XXIst dynasty. The pharaohs who sat on the throne of Tanis in Lower Egypt had as their rivals the High Priests of Amun at Thebes, and in particular Pinudjem I and Pinudjem II. But under the XXIInd dynasty, the realm was reunited. These new pharaohs, of Libyan origin, made Egypt a dynamic power once more, as illustrated by the capture of Jerusalem by Sesonchis I's army. And there was intense maritime and trading activity between the Delta and Asia, via the ports on the Palestinian coast.

The poverty in which historians had supposed that the pharaohs of Tanis lived is disproved not only by the treasures found in their tombs, but also by the royal gifts conferred on certain temples by Osorkon I (924-889), the immediate successor of Sesonchis I. In all, he gave 27,000 kilogrammes of gold and 180,000 kilogrammes of silver to the sanctuaries of the Delta cities. These huge quantities of precious metals came in large part from the treasure he had pillaged in Jerusalem. But whatever their origin, the fact remains that gold and silver were available in abundance in a country once described by scholars as impoverished.

Nothing illustrates more strikingly the intrinsic interest of this period than the beauty of the funerary jewels found at Tanis. In these pieces, there is a renewed vitality, combined with a return, in certain aspects, to traditional forms. The goldwork of Tanis is more restrained than that of Tutankhamun. The "baroque" appearance of the earlier work can be directly attributed to the influence of the religious fervour of the Amarna period. Technically, the Tanite craftsmen were infinitely superior to those who made the rustic earrings of Queen Tausret, the second wife of Sethos II, who reigned briefly at the end of the XIXth dynasty. Furthermore, they were at least the equal of those who worked under the greatest of the Ramessides, in so far as a judgement may be formed from the few surviving objects.

The mummy's amulets

These tiny engraved gold-leaf talismans were worn on necklaces with counterpoises. They represent the soul-bird (above) and the symbols of Upper and Lower Egypt, the uraeus and the vulture (opposite). Height: 3 cm (1¼ in). (Egyptian Museum, Cairo.)

153

6.

The Tanite artefacts do not, then, deserve to be treated conde-
scendingly as belonging to a "transitional" period. The admirable
masks of Psusennes and Wendjebaundjed, and of Sesonchis II,
bear witness to the mastery of the goldsmiths of that time. The
perfection they achieved can also be seen in two famous pieces:
the celebrated triad of Osorkon II, and the magnificent
Karomama in the Louvre, a bronze effigy made by the cire-
perdue method and inlaid with details in gold, electrum and
silver. This second piece represents the Divine Worshipper of
Amun, who was the grand-daughter of Osorkon I.

In any case, whatever the political situation may have been
during the period known as the "Libyan anarchy" (a series of
dynastic quarrels that lasted from the end of the XXIInd dynasty
through the XXIIIrd), these disturbances do not seem to have
adversely affected the quality of artistic production.

A major discovery: ritual vessels

The tombs at Tanis are unique in the history of Egyptian
archaeology, for they are the only such site that has been preserved absolutely intact up to the moment of its discovery. These
graves were never pillaged, and have thus come down to us
complete with their liturgical plate. That found in the tomb of
Psusennes is particularly impressive. In this vault alone, Pierre
Montet counted fourteen vessels in gold and silver. In Tanis as
a whole, some twenty-three vases, ewers, cups, chalices, plates,
bowls, ritual pots and offering tables were found.

Most of these liturgical objects had hitherto only been known
from bas reliefs in temples or tomb paintings. Now, suddenly, the
true perfection of their forms stood revealed. Their restrained

Golden lotus flower chalice

Sitting on an elegant curved stem, the flower of the lotus forms the bowl of this ritual cup. It was certainly used for libations in the tomb in honour of the deceased, but may also have been used during Psusennes' lifetime. It was a gift to the king from Pinudjem, son of Payankh, the high priest of Karnak. Previously, only ceramic versions of such objects were known.
Height: 21.5 cm (8½ in).
(Egyptian Museum, Cairo.)

Opposite, above

A sacrificial jug belonging to the Queen

This curiously shaped jug – a hemispherical body with an inscribed handle and a long spout – bears an inscription in the name of Mutnedjmet, wife of Psusennes I. It was used in the course of funerary ceremonies. Objects of this kind were unknown until the finds at Tanis. This fine piece is in solid gold and measures 30 cm (11¾ in) long.
(Egyptian Museum, Cairo.)

Opposite, below

A gold patera with gadroons and inscribed border

This piece is 16 cm (6¼ in) in diameter. It features a central rosette, from which emerge sixteen gadroons. Around the rim is an inscription to the glory of the king: "Master of the Two Lands, master of the sword, son of Ra, son of Amun: Psusennes".
(Egyptian Museum, Cairo.)

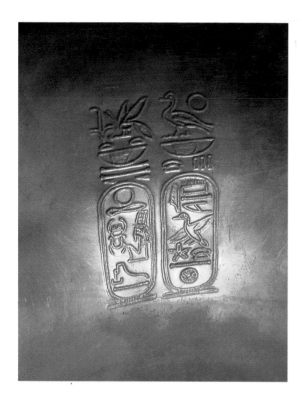

Perfection and variety

Above, detail of the cartouche of Psusennes,
from a broad-lipped vase in solid gold.
This tapered "bowl" was in fact a pendant
to the gold ewer (page 155), as can be seen in
a painting from the tomb of Ramesses III copied
by Rosellini (page 161). The object features
a decorative handle in the form of a lotus flower.
Height: 17 cm (6¾ in).
(Egyptian Museum, Cairo.)

Opposite

This small vase, measuring only 7.7 cm
(3 in) high, has twenty-four gadroons leading up
to a cylindrical neck inscribed with the
cartouches of the king and queen. Despite
its diminutive size, the swollen lip and base add
vigour to the form. (Egyptian Museum, Cairo.)

**Vessels depicted
in tomb paintings**

As well as the vase with handle
and the ewer (seen here on the
left), examples of which have
since been discovered at Tanis,
the elaborate piece on the right
is another original form of which
there are no surviving
specimens. A sphinx sits on
the naos, surrounded by lotus
flowers springing from a
magnificent bowl, decorated
with gadroons. This is one
of several mysterious
"tableware" objects. Copy
by Rosellini, from the tomb
of Ramesses III.

Opposite

Silverware from Tanis

Psusennes' liturgical silverware
consisted of several varieties,
including both bowls and
paterai. Above, a fine drinking
cup, decorated with broken
lines to symbolize water.
The moveable gold handle
is attached by means of rivets.
The lotus rosette features
a central gold stud.
Diameter: 16 cm (6¼ in).
(Egyptian Museum, Cairo.)
Below, a bowl decorated
with a woven motif, bearing
the cartouches of Psusennes,
"first prophet of Amun".
A highly elaborate piece
of silverwork.
Diameter: 14.3 cm (5⅝ in).
(Egyptian Museum, Cairo.)

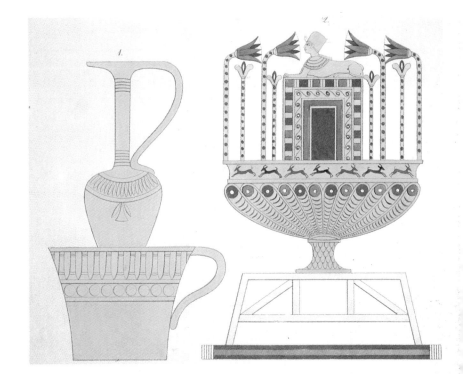

Psusennes' bracelets

Montet found twenty-six
bracelets on Psusennes' mummy.
One of them was a ring of solid
gold, inlaid with large
hieroglyphs in lapis, cornaline,
and turquoise.
Width: 3.8 cm (1½ in).
(Egyptian Museum, Cairo.)

Opposite

The first of these five objects,
a mere 1.8 cm (¾ in) high,
is actually a ring, treated as
a miniature bracelet. The gold
cloisonné work is set with lapis,
cornaline and simplified
cartouches. Above right, an
anklet in two parts with its pin
and clasp. The cloisonné work
represents Khopri. In the centre,
a rigid bracelet made
of seven alternating gold reeds,
four smoothly finished and three
striated. It was dedicated to the
pharaoh by the queen. Below
left, an articulated bracelet with
clasp. The gold reed is decorated
with grecques and with
an inscription of cartouches
inlaid with lapis lazuli. The final
example is also the most
enigmatic. It is in solid gold,
with a triangular section and
weighs 1.75 kg (3lb 14oz).
(Egyptian Museum, Cairo.)

beauty and their plain smooth surfaces, undecorated apart from a brief dedicatory inscription, are a source of wonder to all who set eyes on them. Their very simplicity seems to reveal the sheer immutable brilliance of the gold from which they were fashioned. These objects are almost thirty centuries old, yet they shine forth as if new, freshly created by a craftsman of genius.

They are the product of much patient swageing. They were constantly returned to the fire, in the search for a perfectly balanced outline, modelled on forms that had been prescribed many thousands of years ago. Gold is above all the material that is reserved for the reproduction of traditional forms that were first carved in stone during the pre-dynastic era. Throughout the dynastic era, these forms were perpetuated, as a mark of respect for ancestral liturgical rites and gestures. No finer illustration is to be found of the Egyptian quest for eternity than these vessels, which were used for libations and offerings.

The magnificent jewelry of Psusennes I

Whatever may have been the political and economic situation in the Delta at the beginning of the XXIst dynasty, the geographical context in itself meant that the tombs built there were quite different from the Theban hypogea, as well as from the Old Kingdom mastabas at Giza and Saqqara. The climate at Tanis is determined by the surrounding marshes. Year-round humidity is guaranteed by the many branches of the Nile. The sub-soil is saturated with water; there is not a single patch of raised ground, nor man-made levee, where a tomb guaranteed to remain above water in all circumstances could be built.

Such factors obviously influenced the Ancient Egyptians when they came to build the necropolis at Tanis. The royal tombs are quite small and consist of a simple vault, in the town itself, beside the great temple. Over the graves there must have stood a chapel. The burial chambers are scarcely larger than a sarcophagus. There is no wooden "container" surrounding the stone box, no furniture or apparatus such as beds, cedarwood statues, war chariots, thrones, etc. made from perishable materials. The objects provided for the final journey have been limited to the strict minimum: a coffin, ritual vessels, and jewelry, whether for decoration or to serve as a talisman. The boxes in which these treasures were stacked, and in which hundreds of shabtis accompanied the deceased on his journey to the next life, have utterly disappeared. Everything that is not metal, stone or ceramic has vanished into thin air, including the mummies themselves, of whom only a few bones remain.

Who was Psusennes?

The Pharaoh Psusennes I, second ruler of the XXIst dynasty, reigned from c. 1036 to c. 989 BC. He was the direct contemporary of the high priest, Pinudjem, at Thebes. His reign, which has been classed, rather too hastily, under the "Third Intermediate Period", shows no sign of the sort of decline in power which that rubric would imply. If Egypt was indeed divided, this was a consequence not of Psusennes' weakness, but of the negligence and lack of authority of the last Ramessides to have ruled the country from Upper Egypt.

In the Delta, the drive towards national recovery was obvious. Psusennes created a new capital at Tanis, which, under his rule, became a key port, the hub of an ever-expanding trade with Phoenecia. Whole fleets of ships were soon plying back and forth across the Mediterranean, sailing out from Lake Manzaleh which served to protect the Egyptian port from the labyrinthine marshes of the Delta. Trading agreements with Byblos, Tyre and Sidon gave Egypt access to timber from Mount Lebanon, paid for in turn with gold and silver pitchers, fine linen, papyrus scrolls and manufactured goods.

A magnificent necklace belonging to Psusennes I

This necklace, approximately 35 cm (13¾ in) in diameter, has seven strands made up of five thousand tiny gold disks. The elements out of which it is composed were originally tokens distributed by the king as a reward to deserving subjects. The total weight is 8 kg (17lb 10oz). The large cloisonné clasp is 6.2 cm (2½ in) high (see above) and is stamped with the royal cartouches. Hanging down behind the pharaoh's neck, ten small chains act as counterpoise. These gradually branch out, culminating in a hundred tiny flower-shaped bells. (Egyptian Museum, Cairo.)

Opposite

Magnificent pectorals

The art of the pectoral is
particularly highly developed
in the treasure of Psusennes I.
Above, the front and back of
an openwork pectoral, with gold
cloisonné framing coloured
stones. The form is that of the
naos. A winged solar disk rises
above a lapis lazuli scarab with
multi-coloured wings. On either
side sit the goddesses Isis and
Nephtys. Uraei stand guard
over the royal cartouches.
In the lower frieze, djed pillars
alternate with the emblem of
the reborn sun.
Height: 13 cm (5¹/₈ in).
(Egyptian Museum, Cairo.)
Below: front and back
of a pectoral in the form
of a winged scarab. The wings
are made up of rows of cloisonné
stones crossed with vertical
bands of gold.
Height: 10 cm (4 in).
(Egyptian Museum, Cairo.)

This page

Two details from the scarab
pectoral, with the cartouche
of Psusennes, enlarged to twice
life size. On the front,
the inscription is in inlaid lapis
lazuli. On the back, it is chased
in gold.

The treasure in the tiny vault

In addition, Psusennes began the construction of a huge temple, intended to rival the temple of Amun at Karnak. To this end, he ransacked the ruined buildings of Per-Ramesses for building materials. Per-Ramesses had been built two hundred and fifty years earlier by Ramesses II, and Psusennes had few qualms about confiscating whatever he required, even less so in that he regarded himself as a descendant of the Ramessides. All this activity implies a certain prosperity, of which the treasures found in Psusennes's tomb are eloquent confirmation.

There was more to this treasure than the silver coffin representing the king and the magnificent gold mask (both of which have stylistic affinities with the surviving portraits of Tuthmosis III) and the sumptuous gold and silver ware already described. Many superb pieces of jewelry were also found within the sarcophagus. Although, as an ensemble, they were less impressive than the treasure of Tutankhamun, they certainly do not suggest an ineffectual regime or a period of scarcity. They were literally hundreds of jewels, amulets and talismans, including gold and lapis lazuli necklaces, bracelets set with precious stones, and pendants and rings displaying great novelty and diversity of style.

The various pectorals of Psusennes provide the finest illustration of the beauty and quality of the gold work of this period. They include the straightforward pylon form, with its frame and cavetto cornice, and free variations on the theme of the scarab

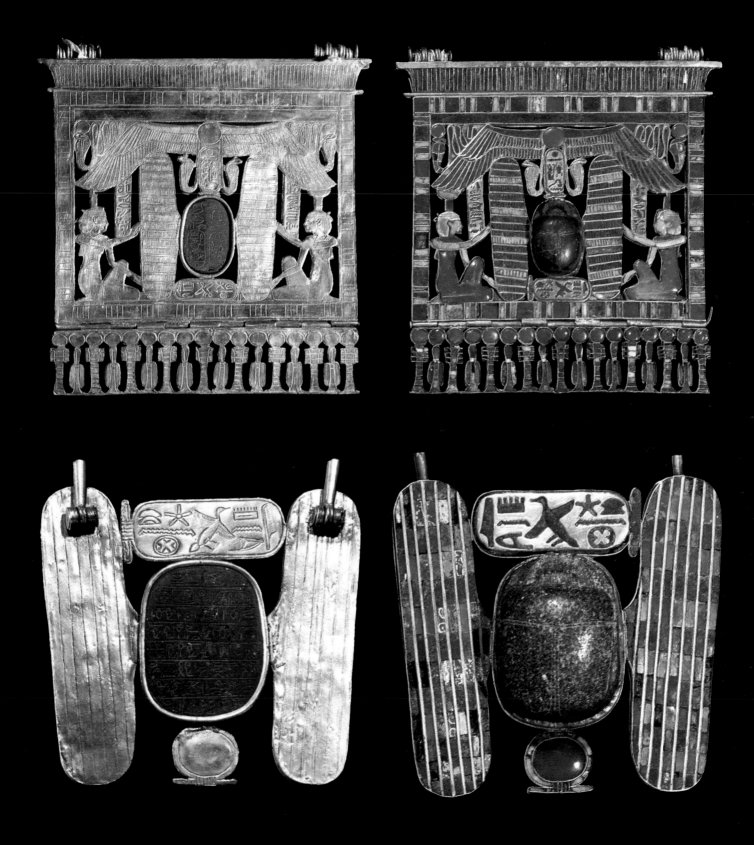

Two dazzling pectorals with their chains

Above, a second pectoral in the form of a scarab. The wings have horizontal polychrome cloisonné worked in lapis, turquoise and cornaline. This is a piece of exceptionally fine quality. The royal cartouche is being pushed by a green jasper scarab. The necklace is made of elongated beads featuring the same materials as the talisman. Height: 10 cm (4 in). (Egyptian Museum, Cairo.)

Below, a pectoral in the form of a temple facade, found on the mummy of Psusennes. It is decorated with two graceful goddesses, Isis and Nephtys, who stretch out their protective wings towards the scarab. The latter is made of organic material, and has partly decomposed. (See enlarged detail on page 5; the entire back is reproduced on page 210.)
Height: 12 cm (4¾ in).
(Egyptian Museum, Cairo.)

Opposite

A hymn of prayer

The back of the black granite scarab seen at the bottom of the preceding page is enlarged here to five times life-size. It is inscribed with a hieroglyphic text – a profession of faith by Psusennes: "My heart is the heart of the sun; the heart of the sun is my heart". The king identifies himself with Ra in order to attain divine immortality.

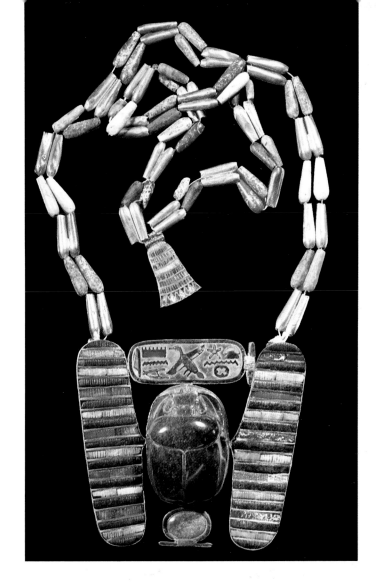

The treasures of the general of the king's archers

Above, a ring with a moving bezel, a design typical of pharaonic art. The ring belonged to Wendjebaundjed, the companion of Psusennes I, and is decorated with a wedjat eye. The talisman is made of amazonite and slotted onto a pin that joins the two ends of the ring proper. (Egyptian Museum, Cairo.)

Opposite

A gold mask of remarkable purity

The burial mask of Wendjebaundjed covered only the face of the head archer's mummy, and featured neither the head-dress nor the necklace found on pharaonc masks. The visual effect of unpolished hammered gold admirably portrays the subject's broad smile and large eyes. Enamel is used solely around the eyes to heighten the gaze. (Egyptian Museum, Cairo.)

with its multi-coloured wings. Their perfection far surpasses anything that has survived from the Ramesside period. They are comparable in quality to the jewelry of Tutankhamun, from which they differ by their more strictly "classical" style.

The brilliance of the graded stones, the minute detail of the cloisonné work, and their formal purity all bear witness to the fact that Tanis must have possessed a gold workshop that was the equal of any that existed in the greatest periods of Egyptian art. Only the Middle Kingdom produced gold work of superior elegance and distinction.

Psusennes sought to emphasise the continuity between his reign and that of his famous predecessors and, accordingly, his tomb harboured many objects from earlier periods which were once again put to good use. One noteworthy surprise was a bronze sacrifical stove that had formerly belonged to Ramesses II. Was this some remote heirloom, or the fruit of recent pillaging in the Valley of the Kings? The second hypothesis seems more likely, and is reinforced by the presence of a fine ritual ewer in gold from the tomb of Ahmose, the founder of the XVIIIth dynasty, who had lived five centuries before Psusennes.

Wendjebaundjed, the eternal companion

The prince Wendjebaundjed belonged to Psusennes's family. He was appointed Head Archer of the king's bodyguard, and general-in-chief of the Egyptian armed forces. He was not only a soldier, but also one of the prophets of Khons at Thebes, and the chief prophet of all the gods. Like General Herihor at Thebes, who had been the first prophet of Amun and had founded a dynasty of priest-kings, Wendjebaundjed's career shows how men who could command the allegiance of both the army and the church might eventually aspire to be the pharoah's alter ego, his virtual equal.

The power that Wendjebaundjed wielded is confirmed by the fact that his tomb was located within the same complex as the pharaoh's own vault. Having served the pharaoh all his life, the prince would thus once more be at his side in the afterworld. His authority is demonstrated by the magnificence of the provisions that surrounded him: a masterful gold mask, and jewelry, of which several pieces were gifts from Psusennes, or from his wife, Mutnedjemet, which they had inherited from a Ramesside "ancestor".

There were also cups and paterai. One of the latter, made of gold and silver, stands out from the group. It depicts women swimming in between fish and lotus flowers, playfully luring ducks into their snares. There are delicate amulets decorated

**Bastet the lionness:
a miniature sculpture**

The goddess carries the solar
disk and the royal uraeus over
her head. Made of solid gold,
with the head of a lionness
and the body of a woman, the
figure is only 9 cm (3½ in)
high. Yet it achieves a real
monumentality, in the same way
as the perfect effigies that make
up the triad of Osorkon II (see
pages 196-197). This piece was
part of the funerary provisions
of Wendjebaundjed, general
of Psusennes's guard.
It functioned as a talisman,
both during the life of its owner,
and after his death.
(Egyptian Museum, Cairo.)

**Isis, goddess of salvation,
companion of the deceased**

Fair Isis, goddess of resurrection,
was laid beside the mummy
of Wendjebaundjed, so as to
intercede in favour of his soul.
This delicate solid gold statuette
hung from a fine gold chain.
It was certainly the work of the
same sculptor-goldsmith who
produced the figure of Bastet
shown opposite. She brings
a delicate feminine touch
to the magical art of ancient
Egypt. Height: 11 cm (4 ⅜ in).
(Egyptian Museum, Cairo.)

A gold and electrum bowl

One of the finest examples
of liturgical ware discovered
at Tanis, this bowl was found
in the tomb of Wendjebaundjed.
It is formed out of large
gadroons, and employs a
technique previously unknown
in the annals of Egyptian art.
The petals of the flowering lotus
are made alternately of gold and
electrum, carefully soldered
together. The resulting form is
almost baroque. The inscription,
wishing the owner "life, health
and strength", is appropriate
for a bowl that would have been
used for libations.
Diameter: 12.7 cm (5 in).
(Egyptian Museum, Cairo.)

with images of Isis or Bastet the cat. There is a miniature golden naos, containing a lapis lazuli statue of Khnum the goat less than two centimetres (³/4 in) high. Perhaps the most surprising of all these pieces is a cup decorated with large gadroons, with alternating petals of gold and silver. The entire collection displays the virtuoso skill of the goldsmiths. The treasures which lay slumbering in this vault until their discovery by Pierre Montet in 1946 are worthy of a great pharaoh.

Amenemipet: the splendour of an obscure pharaoh

The pharaoh Amenemipet, previously unknown to modern scholars, lay buried in the vault originally intended for Psusennes' wife. The tomb intended for him had in all likelihood been sacked, the body hastily transferred to the new sarcophagus and the queen's name erased, save for one surviving cartouche.

Amenemipet was the immediate successor of Psusennes. He reigned briefly in Tanis, from 989 to 981 BC. He seems to have been less wealthy than his predecessor, but this impression may be due to the fact that his initial resting place was pillaged. Whatever the case may be, he left no mask of gold, and his face is known to us only from an anthropomorphic gilded-wood coffin. Although the wood has long since decayed, the form has been preserved thanks to the thin leaf of gold that covered it. This effigy wears the nemes headcloth. The face is highlighted by bronze and enamel eyes, and on the forehead is a magnificent gold uraeus set with precious stones. The sheer perfection of this piece reminds one of the cobra made a thousand years before for Sesostris II, which Petrie had discovered at Illahun.

Among the gold jewelry, two pectorals deserve to be singled out. One of these is decorated on one side with the images of Isis and Nephtys and, on the other, with Khopri's scarab. This openwork piece achieves a remarkable lightness of touch and elegance, balanced by a restrained use of colour. The second pectoral, in contrast, is in solid metal, a style associated with the reigns of Tutankhamun and Ramesses II. The sole decoration, on both sides, is a monochrome repoussé motif, depicting the pharaoh himself standing to make a sacrificial offering to Isis on her throne.

Among the objects that were buried with him, there is also a fine pair of openwork bracelets, bearing the cartouche of Psusennes. Their supple, yet well-balanced forms grow out of the scarab motif, the wings being treated to great effect in cloisonné work as a polychrome chevron.

The most beautiful object in Amenemipet's tomb, however, is without doubt a golden ewer intended for use in the traditional ritual libations. It is made of three parts – a bell-shaped base, an

An obscure ruler and his brief reign

Above, the cartouche of Amenemipet, "beloved of Osiris, master of Abydos", decorating the side of the fine ewer which is seen on page 179.

Opposite

The pharaoh Amenemipet (989-981), who succeeded Psusennes I, was not mentioned in the royal lists. His initial resting place was partially sacked, and his wooden coffin had to be hastily transferred. Thus, he came to share a vault with his predecessor. The coffin is plated with gold leaf, and represents the pharaoh's face. Beneath a splendid gold uraeus, his serene expression is highlighted by forceful bronze eyes and eyebrows. (Egyptian Museum, Cairo.)

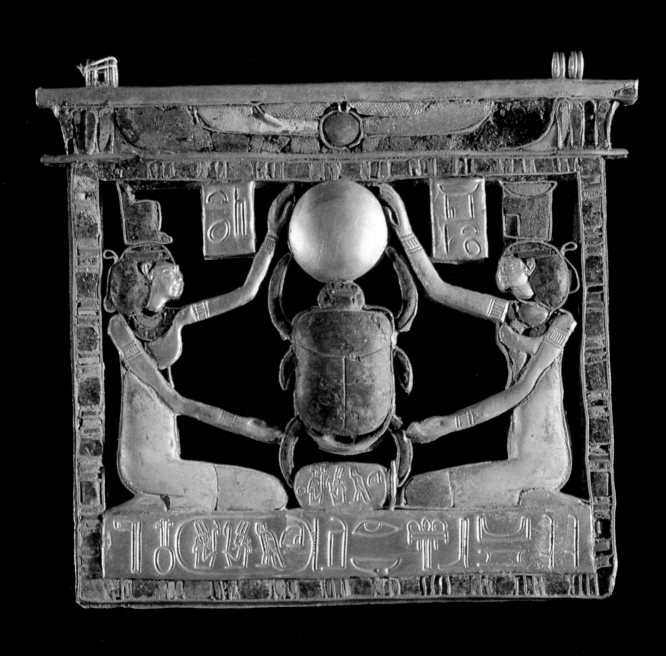

Provisions for an extraordinary journey

Left: although an obscure figure, Amenemipet
still had many fine pieces in his tomb. His
openwork pectoral has great elegance.
Within a frame in the form of a naos, it portrays
the goddesses Isis and Nephtys to either side
of a scarab beetle pushing the solar disk in front
of him. Height: 9.8 cm (3⁷/₈ in).
(Egyptian Museum, Cairo.)
Right: one of the masterpieces of Egyptian
liturgical goldware. This ewer, of a form
previously known only from painted images,
displays all the subtlety and grace that ritual
objects could command. Height: 20 cm (7⁷/₈ in).
(Egyptian Museum, Cairo.)

Religious objects fashioned from silver

Silver was a new addition to the Egyptian artist's
arsenal under the Tanite dynasties. It was
imported from Asia, and often replaced gold in
the making of ritual objects. This page, above:
the squat container has a rimless opening and
a rivetted spout. (The Egyptians had not
mastered the art of soldering silver.) It is
dedicated to Amenemipet, "beloved of Osiris",
the sovereign of the dead. Height: 12.5 cm
(4⁷/₈ in). (Egyptian Museum, Cairo.)

Opposite: This offering stand is made of silver,
as was the equivalent item from Psusennes'
tomb. Its elongated form is enhanced by the
column of text, which reads : "Oh bountiful god,
Amenemipet, Master of the Two Lands, receive
this libation as thine". Height: 41 cm (16¹/₈ in).
(Egyptian Museum, Cairo.)
This page, below: this deeply-chased inscription,
which decorated the edge of the platter, reads:
"Amenemipet, beloved of Osiris, who abides
in his naos". (Egyptian Museum, Cairo.)

oval body and a spout – all soldered together with great skill.
A paragon of elegance featuring, in addition, a discreetly inscribed
royal cartouche, the vase is a masterwork of Egyptian art under
the XXIst dynasty, the equal in all respects of Ahmose's ewer.

Among the silverwork found in the tomb, we should mention
a conical offering table, slightly arched in form, bearing the cartouche of Amenemipet, and a pot-bellied kettle with a spout.
Both are objects which, until the opening of this vault, were
know to Egyptologists only from tomb paintings.

A processional jewel

This unusual miniature palanquin is equipped with carrying rods. Standing on an offering table, it depicts a goddess watching over the pharaoh. Above her head is a falcon, and above the falcon, a flabellum. The structure emerges from a sort of golden enclosure, surmounted by a frieze of uraei; its sides are decorated with a lion and a wild beast with a human head wearing the crown of the Two Lands. Drawing copied by Rosellini from a Theban tomb.

Opposite

Amenemipet's pectoral decorated with chasing and repoussé work

This pendant has a protective function. It is made up of two leaves of gold glued together. Both sides feature a similar thematic motif showing the pharaoh in the act of offering incense to Osiris seated on his throne. The front is simply chased, while the back is treated in heavy repoussé work. Height: 8.8 cm (3½ in). (Egyptian Museum, Cairo.)

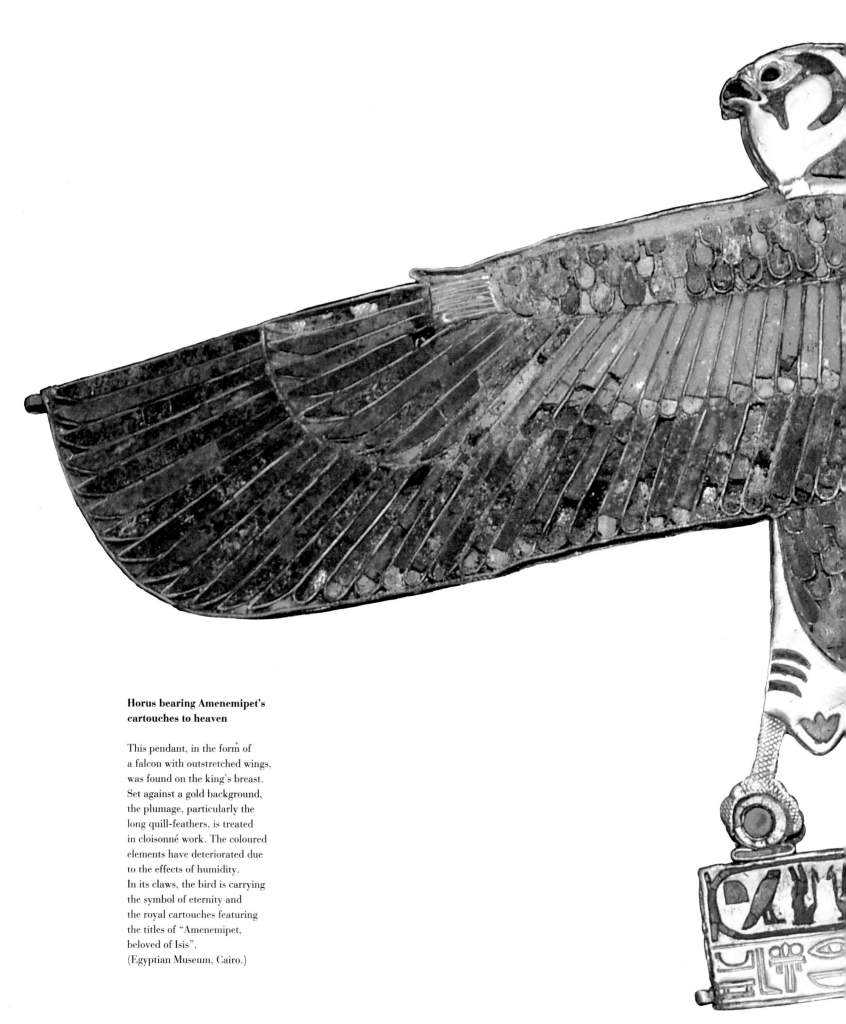

Horus bearing Amenemipet's cartouches to heaven

This pendant, in the form of
a falcon with outstretched wings,
was found on the king's breast.
Set against a gold background,
the plumage, particularly the
long quill-feathers, is treated
in cloisonné work. The coloured
elements have deteriorated due
to the effects of humidity.
In its claws, the bird is carrying
the symbol of eternity and
the royal cartouches featuring
the titles of "Amenemipet,
beloved of Isis".
(Egyptian Museum, Cairo.)

Following pages

**The Libyan king's
sarcophagus and jewelry**

Sesonchis II ruled as co-regent
in c. 890 BC. He was laid to rest
in an unusual solid silver coffin
in the form of a falcon,
representing the pharoah's
transfiguration into sun bird.
As the Egyptians had no
technique for soldering silver,
certain elements,
such as the hands in which
the king clasps the symbolic
sceptres, were rivetted.
(Egyptian Museum, Cairo.)
Opposite: this image of the
goddess Maat spreading her
wings over the cartouche of
Sesonchis II was chased onto
the silver coffin.

Thus, even the most obscure pharaoh of this much-maligned period was laid to rest in a chamber borrowed from his predecessor's wife, and surrounded by vessels and jewelry of the highest quality. These discoveries demonstrate how far the dynasties of Tanis were from marking a low point in Egyptian history.

Sesonchis I and II, and the gold of the Temple of Jerusalem

The first body Montet stumbled upon when he entered the tomb of Psusennes on 18 March 1939 was housed in a silver coffin with a falcon's head. There, in a vestibule measuring four metres by six (thirteen feet by twenty) lay the remains of Sesonchis II, a ruler of the XXIInd dynasty so obscure he was not even mentioned in the List of Kings. This mysterious figure, who ruled as co-regent in around 890 BC, was buried hastily in a tomb where all the chambers were already occupied. Yet he came from an illustrious line: his ancestor Sesonchis I, from Libya, had reigned between 945 and 924 BC. He was known first as High Chief of the Ma, an unruly Libyan tribe which had provided the last rulers of the XXIst dynasty with their personal guard. He acceded to the throne, founding the Sesonchid dynasty which was to restore unity to the Egyptian state, thus making it once again a major power in the Near East.

The biblical books of Kings and of Chronicles relate how Jeroboam had rebelled against Solomon, who wished to put him to death. Jeroboam sought refuge at the court of a pharaoh known in these texts as Shishaq – i.e. Sesonchis I. At the time, relations between Hebrews and Egyptians were cordial, since Solomon had married "the pharaoh's daughter" – the pharaoh, in this case, being Psusennes II.

Sesonchis I's guest doubtless told his host at Tanis of the wealth of the Temple of Jerusalem, and of the palace which Solomon had built. The vast amounts of gold he described must have tempted the Egyptian sovereign. Accordingly, when Jeroboam returned to Jerusalem on Solomon's death and, together with Roboam, divided the Hebrew state into two parts – Juda and Israel – Sesonchis seized the opportunity to launch a raid on the Jewish capital.

What was the treasure of Solomon?

The treasures of the venerable king are described down to the last detail in the Bible. Both the first Book of Kings (7, 13-51) and the second Book of Chronicles (3, 4-5) list the contents of

the Temple of Jerusalem: the golden altar, the table on which the bread was placed in offering, fine gold candelabras, gold flowers, lamps and snuffers, basins, sacrificial knives, ewers, censors of solid gold and the golden hinges of the Holy of Holies and the House of Yahweh. There were also the gifts that David had made to the Temple – gold and silver, and massive vases. These gifts are described in the first book of Chronicles (ch 29): three thousand talents of gold of Ophir, and seven thousand talents of silver, to which David's officers added five thousand talents of gold and a thousand talents of silver.

The Book of Chronicles also tells us that Solomon had painted the interior of the Temple with pure gold, and had gold-plated the cypress-wood walls. He covered the entire House in gold: its beams, doorsteps, walls and doors. The decoration of the Holy of Holies alone cost a total of six hundred talents of pure gold. The nails weighed fifty shekels. There were gold cherubim. If we reckon that a shekel weighed 680 grammes (24 oz) and a talent of 60 minas, 818.5 grammes (29 oz), it involved some 30 tonnes (37 tons) of gold.

In addition, Solomon had placed the Ark of the Covenant in the Temple, with its cherubim forged from solid gold, as well as the gold shields that had been captured from Hadadezer.

Finally, Solomon's palace also contained extensive decorations in gold, in particular the armour of the king's pretorian guard. The second Book of Chronicles (chapter 9) mentions two hundred large shields of hammered gold, each of which weighed six hundred gold shekels, as well as three hundred small gold shields each covered with three minas of gold. This armour alone was equivalent to over two and a half tons of gold.

What was the origin of all this gold? Apparently it came from the same sources as did the gold of the pharaohs: the southern part of the Red Sea. When the Queen of Sheba visited Solomon, she is said to have brought with her one hundred and twenty gold talents, as well as perfumes and spices.

It is easy to understand how the ruler of Tanis might have been envious of such wealth. And then the division of the Jewish state into two parts brought that wealth within the grasp of his armies.

The Bible estimates that the Pharaonic army was made up of one thousand two hundred war chariots and sixty thousand horses – incredible numbers, doubtless intended to explain the defeat of the Hebrews. The Egyptians crossed the Sinai, took control of Juda and marched into Jerusalem. They did not punish the people, but concentrated on confiscating the treasure of the Temple and the palace. The booty they brought back with them to Tanis was a splendid haul. The Bible itself describes the success of their raid: "So Shishak king of Egypt came up against Jerusalem,

The jewels of Sesonchis II

This gold pectoral in the form of a sanctuary facade comes from the treasure of Sesonchis II. Beneath the cavetto cornice bearing the emblem of a winged sun, a second similar symbol is featured over a centrally-placed green stone scarab with outspead wings. The scarab is flanked by two kneeling goddesses (Isis and Nephtys) who offer him their protection. Height: 15.6 cm (6⅛ in). (Egyptian Museum, Cairo.)

Opposite

A curious pectoral, composed of a lapis lazuli scarab pushing the disk of the sun between two uraei, each wearing the crown of Upper Egypt. Attached to the base is an articulated plaque decorated with lotus flowers. Height: 7 cm (2¾ in). (Egyptian Museum, Cairo.)

**Sesonchis II clad head
to foot in precious metal**

Above: the supremely beautiful
gold mask of Sesonchis II, like
that of Wendjebaundjed, only
covered his face and features
neither nemes nor gorget. The
treatment of the eyes and faintly
smiling lips give the pharaoh an
air of superiority. This is
a magnificent portrait in thick
gold leaf, worked by swageing.
Unfortunately, the original
enamel highlighting
the eyebrows and pupils
has disappeared.
(Egyptian Museum, Cairo.)

Below: Like Psusennes,
Sesonchis II wore gold sandals
in his coffin. The design is both
original and practical, inspired
by models in common use
at the time.
Length: 29 cm. (11³/₈ in)
(Egyptian Museum, Cairo.)

and took away the treasures of the house of the Lord, and the treasures of the king's house; he took all: he carried away also the shields of gold which Solomon had made" (II Chronicles 12).

This exemplary act of pillage explains the magnificence of the XXIInd dynasty and the fabulous gifts that Osorkon I was able to make to the temples of the Delta cities (27 tonnes – 26 imperial tons – of gold and 180 tonnes – 177 imperial tons – of silver). It also explains where the great treasures came from which were laid beside the remains of Sesonchis II in his makeshift tomb in Tanis.

A mask of solid gold

"The chamber was chock full of objects", wrote Montet: "hundreds of funerary statuettes (or shabtis), ten canopic vases, bronze tools and accessories". The unusual form of the silver coffin in the effigy of a falcon, the symbol of Horus and of Sokar, took the explorers by surprise. The coffin, like that of Psusennes I, was made entirely from solid silver and decorated with fine chasing. All the separate pieces, such as the sceptre, flail, hands, were fixed by rivets, because Egyptian craftsmen had not developed a technique for soldering silver.

When Montet lifted the lid of the coffin on 21 March 1939, he discovered a second coffin within. This second coffin was made of boards, and partially covered with fine gold leaf. It too was in the form of a falcon. As soon as he looked inside, Montet saw that it contained "jewelry in excellent condition", even though the mummy itself had not survived.

Montet was struck above all by the beauty of the gold mask – "a veritable work of art". Unlike the mask of Psusennes, which surrounded the whole head, this one covered only the face, in a similar fashion to that of Wendjbauendjed, with which it also had many technical and stylistic affinities. In both cases the object had been fashioned from a thick sheet of gold using the hammer-work technique of swageing. The face was finely proportioned, with delicate features, a full-lipped, almost smiling mouth and a straight, faintly aquiline nose. Owing to the humidity of the vault, the eyes and eyebrows had lost the coloured paste insertions that must once have enlivened the facial appearance.

The craftsmen who made masks for the rulers of Tanis eschewed the brilliant polishing and the sheer mirror-like surface that characterise the mask of Tutankhamun. Instead, they preferred a restrained matt finish. Occasionally, as in the case of Psusennes, the hammer marks were left visible, so as to bring the surface to life by imparting to it a barely perceptible vibration. This was undoubtedly a result of stylistic choice rather than

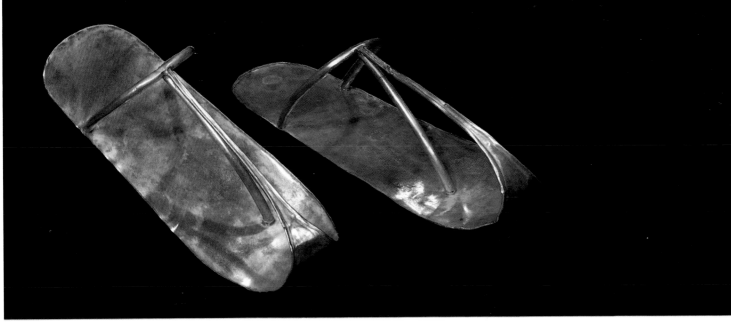

Jewels of great purity from the time of Sesonchis II

Sesonchid jewelry marks one of the supreme achievements in the history
of Egyptian goldwork. Below, a bracelet decorated with a wedjat eye
that belonged to Sesonchis I (945-924 BC). It was found in the grave
of his descendant, Sesonchis II. As can be seen in the detail opposite,
the highly stylised lapis lazuli cloisonné work is imbued with great expressive
force. Diameter: 6.5 cm (2½ in). (Egyptian Museum, Cairo.)

Opposite, above: Bracelet belonging to Sesonchis II, with a lapis lazuli scarab.
The ring proper teminates on either side in an elegant papyrus umbel.
Diameter: 6.5 cm (2½ in). (Egyptian Museum, Cairo.)
Below: This gold bracelet belonging to Sesonchis II, with its decorative
Mesopotamian lapis lazuli cylinder, indicates the pharaonic taste
for "exotic" jewelry. The cylinder, engraved fifteen centuries before
the bracelet itself was made, depicts the legendary theme of Gilgamesh killing
wild animals. Maximum diameter: 7.7 cm (3 in). (Egyptian Museum, Cairo.)

192

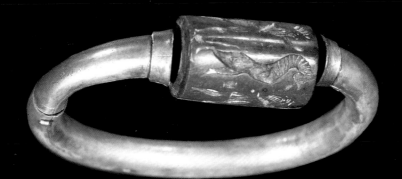

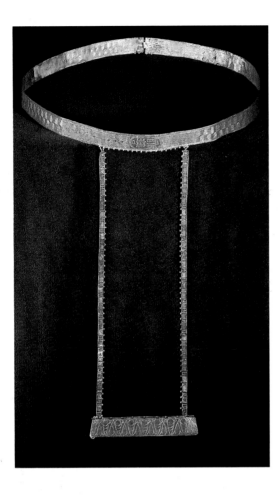

**An unusual item of liturgical dress featuring
a gold armature**

This gold belt, whose frame used to support
the pharaoh's ceremonial apron made of multi-
coloured beads, was found on the mummy
of Sesonchis II. Such ritual apparel was worn
by the pharaoh when he officiated in the temple
and often features in frescoes (see page 135).
Height: 40 cm (15¾ in).
(Egyptian Museum, Cairo.)

Opposite

Pectoral with the solar bark

This pectoral was found in the tomb of Sesonchis
II. It represents the solar bark sailing across the
primordial ocean under the protection of Hathor
and Maat. This jewel was already in Sesonchis I's
possession prior to his ascent to the throne,
at a time when he was still Commander
of the Meshwesh, the Libyan soldiers who formed
the royal guard. Width: 7.8 cm (3 in).
(Egyptian Museum, Cairo.)

any technical shortcoming, for we have highly polished pieces
dating from exactly the same period. The goldsmiths of Tanis
deliberately sought out the subdued gleam of beaten gold for the
portraits they made of their pharaohs.

The jewelry of the dead

Together with this splendid mask, Sesonchis II took with him
into the tomb an exceptional collection of jewelry: fingerstalls,
golden sandals (quite unlike those of Psusennes), a gold belt with
a rigid apron, as if intended for sacrificial use, numerous amulets
and weapons, and countless bracelets and necklaces, as well as
talismans in the form of pectorals.

Some of these pieces – and not the least important – were inherited from Sesonchis I. These include a superb rigid cylindrical
bracelet, whose articulated form represents a wedjat eye in lapis
lazuli cloisonné work. There is also a pectoral depicting Amun's
boat flanked on either side by the guardian goddesses Maat and
Hathor. This piece, of exceptional quality, bears an inscription
mentioning Sesonchis, described as the Great Chief of Ma, at a
time when he had not yet ascended to the throne of Tanis. This in
no way detracts from the perfection of the piece, and provides
additional evidence of the stature of the future pharaoh.

Tanis revisited

This brief survey of the goldwork of the rulers of the two
Tanite dynasties (the XXIst and XXIInd) should suffice to show
that this was far from having been a period of decline in the history of Egypt. The funerary jewelry that we have studied is the
product of an art that had achieved aesthetic and technical mastery, practised in a prosperous land. For Egypt was in fact expe-
riencing a phase of renewal. Trade with her neighbours was
expanding, thanks to her renowned merchant fleet. Military campaigns could be conducted swiftly and successfully, thanks to her
chariot divisions. The Delta had been reunited with Upper Egypt,
and the High Priests of Amun had submitted to the authority of
the Libyan dynasty. Solomon's monopoly on commerce with
Arabia had been overturned. The canal that joined the
Mediterranean to the Red Sea had been re-opened, thus facilita-
ting the import-export trade. Furthermore, with her mounting
reserves of silver and gold, the country could justifiably boast of
being the leading banker to international commerce.

This knowledge we owe to the discoveries made by Montet at
Tanis, discoveries which have served to rehabilitate a long-
neglected period of Egyptian history, and to reveal the outstanding achievements of the goldsmiths of the Delta.

LATE PERIOD GOLDWORK :
FROM Pinudjem TO THE Ptolemies

This superb pendant representing a triad of gods – Horus, Osiris and Isis,
grouped on the same gold base – dates from the reign of Osorkon II.
It is one of the treasures of the Louvre.

Opposite

A marvel of Tanite art: the triad of Osorokon II

This detail, less than 4 cm (1½ in) high, shows
Osiris, framed by the protective hands of Horus
and Isis, crouching on a lapis lazuli pillar, wearing
the white crown and the feathers of Maat, together
with a false beard. (The Louvre, Paris.)

The final period of Egyptian civilisation spans one and a half
millennia, from the Tanite dynasties to the closing of the temple
of Isis at Philae, in 537 BC. The task of providing an overview of
such a lengthy period would prove difficult, even if substantial
archaeological evidence of its main stages were to have survived.
Excepting the treasure of Tanis, however, scarcely any other
tombs of this period have been found intact with their jewelry
and gold. As a rule, all that has come down to us through a
haphazard series of discoveries are isolated objects, whose original context has, in most cases, remained a sealed book.

Among those jewels which date from the two Tanite dynasties,
but which were not part of Montet's discoveries, we should

Following pages

The sphinx of King Siamun of Tanis

Enlarged four times, this small sphinx with a
human head and lion's body dates from the reign
of Siamun (976-958), during the XXIst dynasty
at Tanis. It is made of bronze, probably using
the cire perdue method, and inlaid with gold
and silver. It holds out an offering to the gods
on a platter stamped with the royal cartouche.
Length: 10.3 cm (4 in). (The Louvre, Paris.)

The fair Karomama, divine worshipper of Amun at Karnak

The art of bronze working flourished during the XXIInd dynasty (between 870 and 825 BC). The virtuoso perfection which it ultimately attained is well illustrated by this statue of Karaomama, acquired by Champollion at Thebes in 1829. Standing 60 cm (23½ in) high, it is a unique object. The bronzework offers a display of consummate craftsmanship, while the pink and yellow gold and electrum inlay work is exquisite. The shoulders are entirely draped in a broad, highly worked gorget. The body-hugging dress with its pleated sleeves is embellished with a traditional motif featuring the wings of deities. (The Louvre, Paris.)

mention certain pieces now in the collection of the Louvre: a golden necklace with a bunch of tiny bells and chains that belonged to the priest-king Pinudjem of Thebes; a bronze sphinx with embedded gold highlights, representing the pharaoh Siamun (975-959 BC); and the superb triad of Osorkon II (874-850 BC), which is one of the absolute masterpieces of Tanis. It is made up of three solid gold statuettes grouped on a single pedestal: the figures of Horus and Isis stand to either side of a lapis lazuli pillar on which the figure of Osiris crouches, as if ready to be reborn.

Besides these three pieces in the Louvre, we should mention another important object held in the Cairo museum: the pectoral of Osorkon III, discovered in 1915 at Tell el-Moqdam, and which belonged to Queen Kama of Taremu (Leontopolis). This, again, features three figures: two goddesses, Maat, emblem of justice and harmony, and the heavenly Hathor, and in between them a god in the form of a ram, made of lapis lazuli and crowned with a disk of gold, symbolising the sun emerging from a lotus flower in the first dawn of the world.

Bronze statues

However, in terms of sheer metalworking crafstmanship, the most brilliant creations of the Late Period are certainly its bronze statues. In addition, these works are characterised by the emergence of a new theme: that of the priests and the "divine worshippers of Amun", treated as full-length figures. The craftsmen of that time produced many marvelous pieces featuring this theme, probably using the cire perdue method.

The finest example of this technique is the 60 cm (2')-high statue of Karomama, representing a lady of noble birth who lived at the time of Osorkon II and Takelot II (between 870 and 825 BC). She was of royal blood, being the grand-daughter of the pharaoh Osorkon I, and was apparently buried in the Ramesseum at Thebes. Champollion acquired this bronze statue of her at Karnak in 1829.

The statue offers a sublimely idealised image of the queen, "wife of god and mistress of the Two Lands". Her delicate forms are tightly wound in a sheath dress with a broad belt, and are decorated all over by the protective wings of the heavenly goddess, Nut. The details are defined by silver, pink gold and electrum wire inlaying. Subtle patterns of folded material confer a delicate sense of movement to the bust and the broad sleeves. The shoulders and neck are covered by a large many-tiered necklace. This is an accurate representation of the kind of large multi-coloured glass bead necklaces so popular in Egypt. The face has

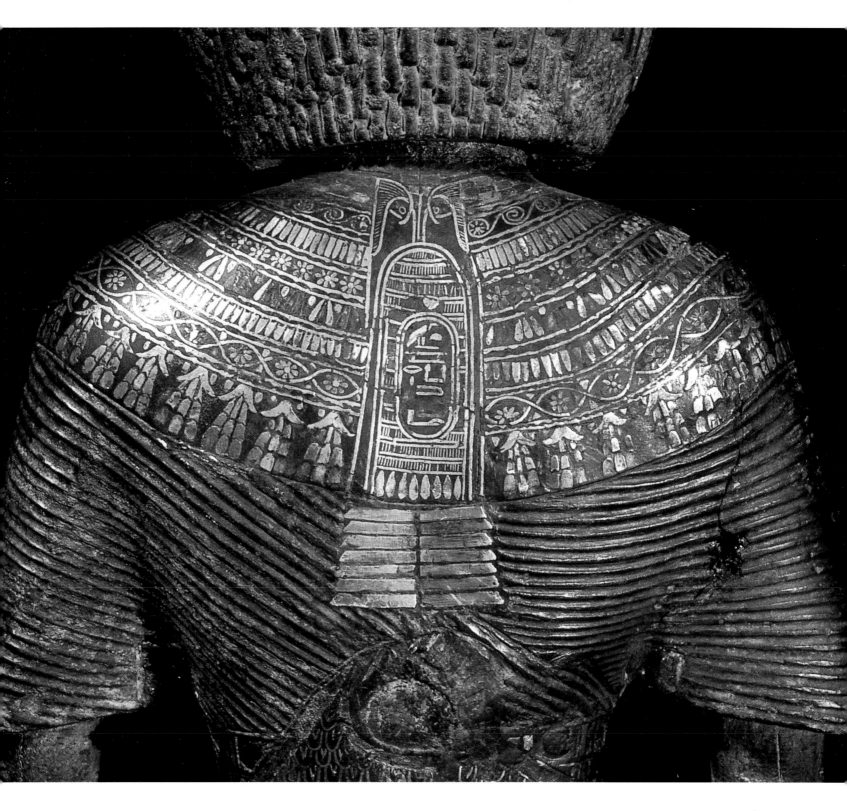

The splendid gold necklace of Karomama

This rear-view detail from the statue of Karomama highlights the polychrome inlay
work used to represent the seven-stranded gorget. The broad clasp-cum-counterpoise
is decorated with the cartouche of the divine worshipper, a princess with considerable
power and influence over both religious and political matters. (The Louvre, Paris.)

fine features, large elongated eyes, and a thin mouth. The head is held in a hieratic pose at the top of her long neck. Her brow is framed by a thick square wig, and crowned by the royal uraeus. Originally, she held in her hands an offering to Amun – a necklace, perhaps, or a pendant. For this beautiful lady would have been standing before the holy naos of the sanctuary of Amun at Karnak, in the temple where she had come to make an important offering.

The "Ethiopian" and Greek periods

From 730 BC onwards, the kingdom of Napata held sway over Egypt through the Kushite dynasty. This dominance is reflected in a group sculpture to be found in the Louvre. It is made up of two elements: a bronze statuette of Taharqa (690-664 BC), a Nubian ruler, kneeling as he makes an offering of perfume, and the god Hemen to whom he prays, in the form of a falcon made of gold-plated schist.

The period which followed has left too little evidence for us to be able to define the evolution of its art with any degree of certainty. The one exception to this rule is the treasure of the queen Amanishakheto of Meroë, which dates from the first century BC. It was discovered in 1834 in her pyramid by the Italian Giuseppe Ferlini. Drastic demolition work was necessary in order finally to remove it, and in the process Ferlini substantially damaged this important monument.

The fine gold jewelry which he retrieved by this act of vandalism formed a coherent ensemble of great intrinsic interest. Ferlini quickly sold them in lots to the museums in Munich and Berlin. There Richard Lepsius admired them, and later included them in his monumental work published between 1849 and 1859. Unfortunately, part of the treasure housed in Berlin was lost at the end of the Second World War.

The interest of this collection lies in the persistence of the pharaonic forms in a peripheral zone of the Egyptian empire at a very late date. The symbols and the talismanic character of these Meroitic jewels are very similar to those which were to be found in the land of Egypt some two thousand years earlier.

It was at this period that the pharaonic art of working gold, as represented in reliefs in Ptolemaic temples, began to face increasing competition from the Hellenic aesthetic. There were now two artistic schools vying for the favours of the public: that influenced by the Achemenid style, which had spread to Egypt from Persia since the time of Cyrus, and that which used the language of Greek art and craft, which had been imported by the Lagides.

Ring belonging to Hormes, Minister of Osorkon II

Like the scarab or wedjat eye featuring on certain Egyptian rings (see page 170), this rectangular green feldspar bezel could pivot on its axis. It belonged to Hormes, Inspector-General and royal scribe. (The Louvre, Paris.)

Opposite

Karomama and her missing sistrums

Karomama's fine-featured face, with inlaid almond-shaped eyes, appears beneath a large wig. Her slender neck and shoulders are covered by a massive gold necklace, while the profile of her breasts is visible beneath the pleats of a belted linen dress. She holds out both hands, as if proffering a gift or shaking sistrums in honour of Amun. (The Louvre, Paris.)

Hathor and Maat worshipping the goat Khnum

This pectoral was found in the Delta in 1915 in a tomb at Tell el Moqdam,
formerly known as Leontopolis. It belonged to the mother of Osorkon III,
Queen Kama (c. 800 BC). The god Khnum, made of lapis lazuli, is depicted
emerging from a bouquet of lotus flowers and surmounted by a disk
representing the nocturnal sun. He is flanked by the standing figures
of the goddesses Hathor and Maat. Height: 11.7 cm (4⅝ in).
(Egyptian Museum, Cairo.)

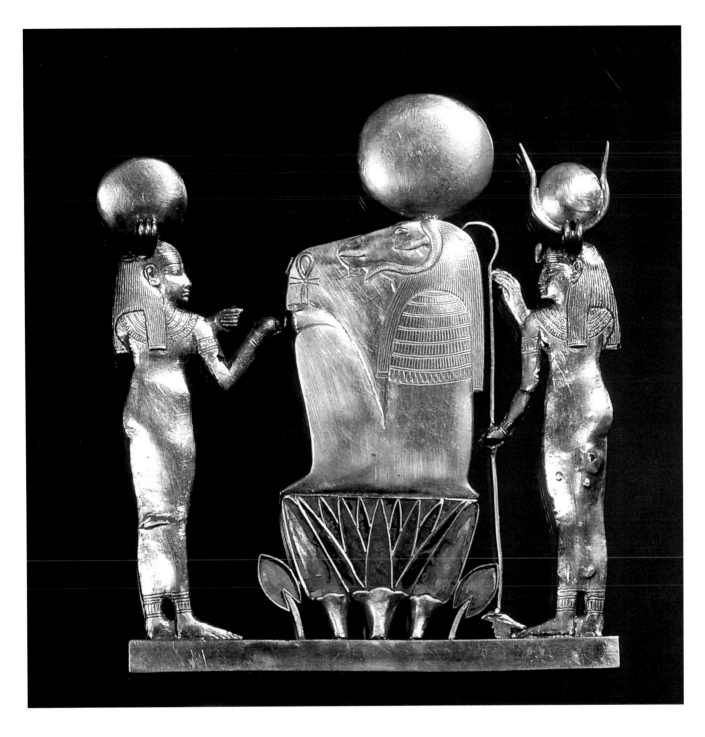

An unusual assymetrical composition

The reverse of the pectoral-talisman from Tell el Moqdam is made entirely
of gold. The sole note of colour is introduced by the floral cloisonné elements.
The composition is remarkable for its elegance and assymetry. The rarety
of such designs only adds to the aesthetic interest of this piece.
(Egyptian Museum, Cairo.)

**The pharaoh Taharka making
an offering to the falcon Hemen**

On a base of silver-plated schist,
this work combines the bronze
effigy of the kneeling pharaoh
holding two ointment vases,
with a large gold falcon
representing Hemen. Taharka
(690-664) was a ruler of the
XXVth Kushite or Meroitic
dynasty. He is portrayed, wearing
a simple apron and a diadem with
a uraeus, performing a ritual
which reenacts one of the most
ancient of Egyptian traditions.
Height: 19.7 cm (7¼ in).
(The Louvre, Paris.)

Henceforth, Egyptian goldwork was no longer determined by
the values and forms of pharaonic art. It was superseded by the
Greco-Roman aesthetic, failing to put up the resistance that was
shown by Egyptian architecture, and to which the last great
temples built in Upper Egypt under the rule of the Roman
Empire bear witness.

Jewelry lost the religious significance that it had hitherto possessed, even before the indigenous forms of worship were fully
extinct. Instead, it became a luxury item, a form of ornamentation for the ruling elite, a readily marketable commodity subject
to the whims of "fashion". This change of function brought with
it a profound formal revolution. The last traces of the art of the
Pharaohs were swept away.

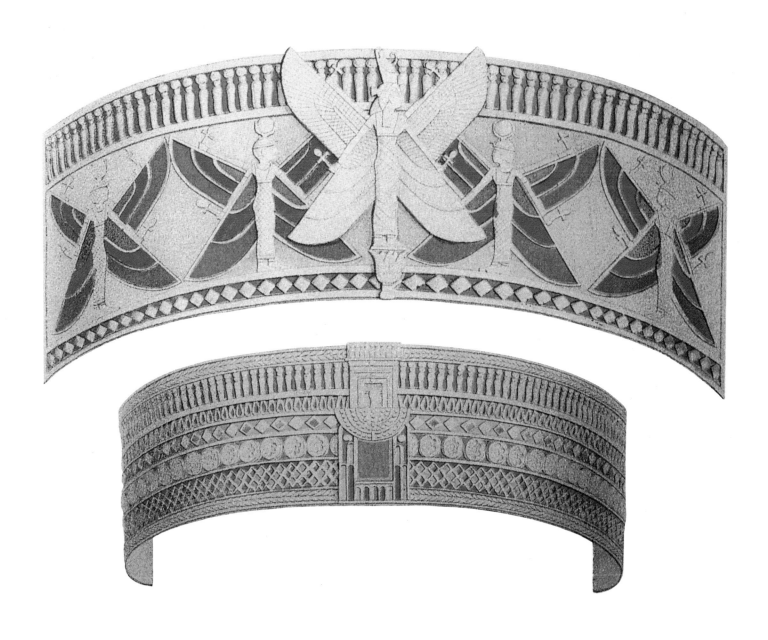

**Remains of the treasure
of a Meroitic queen**

The jewelry of Queen
Amanishakheto was discovered
in 1834 in a pyramid at Meroë,
in present-day Sudan,
by Giuseppe Ferlini. These
pieces attracted the attention
of Lepsius, who drew these two
gold and enamel bracelets. They
illustrate the survival of
Egyptian technique as late
as the first century BC.

207

CONCLUSION

This fine sheet of gold decorated in repoussé work, along with its accompanying lapis lazuli tablet, come from a deposit of donations of Ptolemy IV Philopator (222-205 BC) discovered at the temple of Mut at Tanis. (The Louvre, Paris.)

Previous pages

Remains from the tomb of the high priest Hornakht

The sarcophagus of Prince Hornakht, a son of Osorkon II (874-850 BC) and high priest of Amun, was pillaged in ancient times. His grave lay close to that of his father at Tanis. It was not, however, stripped of all its treasure; the thieves, who had bored a hole through the granite, were unable to steal certain small amulets which were sewn to the mummy for protection in the afterworld. There were duly discovered by Montet on removal of the bulky coffin lid. They are formed of small sheets of gold decorated with cloisonné work in lapis and green paste. Left, the effigy of Osiris, god of the dead; above him, the vulture symbolising the sky, and the mummified falcon Akhem. Below, wings outspread, a bird representing the soul of the deceased in the process of being reborn. Height of Osiris: 8 cm (3⅛ in).
(Egyptian Museum, Cairo.)

In this book, I have presented a survey of the goldwork created in the valley of the Nile over a period spanning several millennia. Despite the limited number of masterpieces that have by chance survived, the overall impression that emerges is, I hope, one of great magnificence and of outstanding creativity.

Egypt built temples and tombs of unparalleled splendour, fit to receive the prayers and worship of its rulers and its noble elite. Yet in the miniature art of jewelry, it may well have surpassed all its other achievements, thanks to the talent of those artists who were able to transpose the formal vocabulary of the most grandiose creations into the delicate idiom of precious metals. Thus the smallest ornament, pectoral or talisman, was endowed with a monumental force, an almost architectural presence, which placed it on an equal footing with the grandest of religious edifices.

Opposite

Gold, the prestigious symbol of eternity

This pectoral of Psusennes I (for a rear-view of this object, see page 169) illustrates the superb quality of the work of the Tanite goldsmiths. The delicate effigies of Isis and Nephtys protect the cartouches of the king in the afterworld.
(Egyptian Museum, Cairo.)

The goddess of Philae wearing heavy jewels

Few traces of goldwork from the Ptolemaic period (305-30 BC) have survived. Evidence pointing to the continuation of the pharaonic style comes from temple bas reliefs. Here, the image of the fair goddess of salvation is featured on the facade of the first pylon of the temple of Isis at Philae. She is wearing a gorget and an upper-arm bracelet decorated with rosettes.

In creating idealised portraits of their rulers, radiant, ever-young and utterly serene, these craftsmen rivalled the finest sculptors of any period, and conferred a kind of eternity upon their kings. They showed how gold could transmute the remains of the dead into an immortal image and impart to their features a liveliness that would help ressuscitate them in the afterworld. In this world of everlasting delight, eulogised in their religion's hymns, the forms of men would at last be clothed in the "flesh of the gods".

**The muted glister of gold
on the temple walls**

The apse of the same sanctuary
at Philae features reliefs – from
a later date and more crudely
executed – in which Isis
is depicted wearing a broad
necklace and two upper-arm
bracelets. One of these is
decorated with a key of life set
between two wedjat eyes. Gold
and jewelry continued to exercise
their mysterious and subtle sway
over the Egyptians' artistic
imagination.

Gold and lapis lazuli: a necklace belonging to Psusennes I

This two-stranded necklace is made of alternating cylindrical beads of gold
and lapis lazuli. It was found in the tomb of the great Tanite pharaoh.
The clasp bears the royal cartouche. (Egyptian Museum, Cairo.)

FURTHER READING

ALFRED, Cyril, *Jewels of the Pharaohs, Egyptian Jewellery of the Dynastic Period*, London, 1971.

ANDREWS, Carol, *Ancient Egyptian Jewellery*, British Museum Publications, London, 1990.

CAPART, Jean, *Tout-Ankh-Amon*, Brussels, 1943.

CARTER, Howard, and A. C. Mace, *The tomb of Tut-Ankh-Amen Discovered by the late Earl of Carnarvon and Howard Carter*, photos Harry Burton, 3 volumes, London, 1923, 1927, 1933.

DAUMAS, François, *La civilisation de l'Egypte pharaonique*, Paris, 1965.

DESROCHES-NOBLECOURT, Christiane, *Vie et mort d'un pharaon : Toutankhamon*, Paris, 1967.

Dictionnaire de la civilisation égyptienne, by Georges POSENER *et alii*, Paris, 1959.

EDWARDS, I.E.S., *The Treasures of Tutankhamun*, London, 1972.

FLINDERS, Petrie, Sir, *Lahun II*, British School of Archaeology in Egypt, London, 1923.

HOVING, Thomas, *Tout-Ankh-Amon, Histoire secrète d'une découverte*, Paris, 1979.

La femme au temps des pharaons, Exhibition, Munich 1985, catalogue by Dietrich Wildung, Mainz, 1985.

LECLANT, Jean, general editor, *Le monde égyptien*, in the series, *L'univers des formes* : I. *Le temps des pyramides*, Paris, 1978 ; II. *L'empire des conquérants*, Paris, 1979 ; III. *L'Egypte du crépuscule*, Paris, 1980. Chapters on goldwork by Christiane Desroches-Noblecourt.

MONTET, Pierre, *La nécropole royale de Tanis*, 3 volumes, I. *Les constructions du tombeau d'Osorkon II à Tanis*, Paris, 1947 ; II. *Les constructions et le tombeau de Psousennès à Tanis*, Paris, 1951; III *Les constructions et le tombeau de Chéchonq à Tanis*, Paris, 1960.

MONTET, Pierre, *Tanis, douze années de fouilles dans une capitale oubliée du Delta égyptien*, Paris, 1942.

MORGAN, J. de, *Fouilles à Dahchour, mars-juin 1894*, with a prefatory notice by Gustave Jéquier, Vienna, 1895.

REEVES, Nicholas, *The Complete Tutankhamun, The King, The Tomb, The Royal Treasure*, London, 1990.

STIERLIN, Henri, *Egypte, des origines à l'islam*, Paris, 1984.

STIERLIN, Henri, et Christiane Ziegler, *Tanis, trésors des pharaons*, preface by Jean Leclant, Freiburg-Paris, 1987.

Tanis, l'or des pharaons, Exhibition, Paris 1987, catalogue with texts and notes by Jean Leclant, Jean Yoyotte, Christiane Ziegler and Jean-Louis de Cénival, Paris, 1987.

Treasures of Tutankhamun, Exhibition at the National Gallery of Art, 1976, description of the exhibits by I.E.S. Edwards, New York, 1976.

VERNIER, Emile, "Bijoux et orfèvrerie", in *Catalogue général des antiquités égyptiennes du musée du Caire*, 3 volumes, Cairo, 1907-1909-1927.

VERNIER, Emile, "La bijouterie et la joaillerie égyptiennes", in *Mémoires publiés par les membres de l'Institut français d'archéologie orientale du Caire*, vol. II, 1907.

WILDUNG, Dietrich, *L'âge d'or de l'Egypte : le Moyen Empire*, Freiburg, 1984.

WILKINSON, A., *Ancient Egyptian Jewellery*, London, 1971.

Evening light on a relief of Isis at the Ptolemaic temple of Kom Ombo. Traces of stucco can be made out on the sculpted stone. The stucco originally would have been painted, creating a polychrome effect in the architectural decor surrounding the goddess adorned in her gold bracelets, gorget and head-dress.

M~AP~

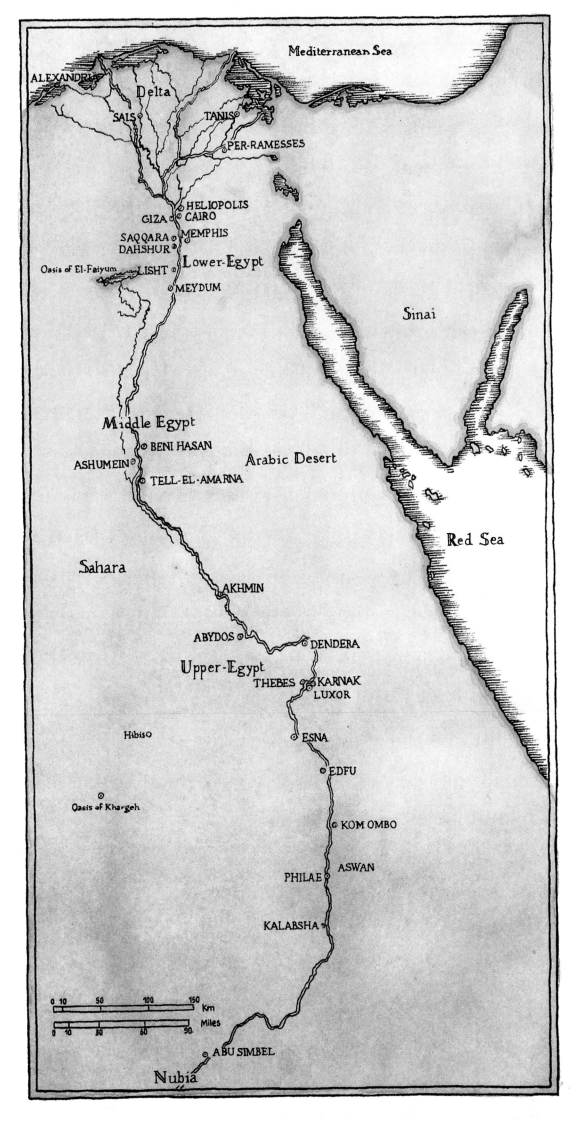

Mediterranean Sea

ALEXANDRIA

Delta

SAIS

TANIS

PER-RAMESSES

HELIOPOLIS
GIZA CAIRO
SAQQARA MEMPHIS
DAHSHUR
Oasis of El-Faiyum LISHT Lower-Egypt
MEYDUM

Sinai

Middle Egypt
BENI HASAN
ASHUMEIN
TELL-EL-AMARNA

Arabic Desert

Sahara

AKHMIN

Red Sea

ABYDOS DENDERA
Upper-Egypt
THEBES KARNAK
LUXOR

Hibis ESNA

EDFU

Oasis of Khargeh

KOM OMBO

ASWAN
PHILAE

KALABSHA

0 10 50 100 150
Km
Miles
0 10 30 60 90

ABU SIMBEL

Nubia

Glossary

Akhenaten: "He with whom the Disk is pleased". Name taken by the pharaoh Amenophis IV (1372-1354) during the movement of religious and theological reform which he instigated.

Alloy: a mixture of two or more metals, produced by their fusion. The melting temperature of an alloy is lower than those of the metals of which it is composed.

Amarna: from Tell el-Amarna, the Arabic name of the site of Akhetaten. As adjective, qualifies both the period and the artistic style of the heresy of Amenophis IV.

Amenophis IV, see under Akhenaten.

Amun: Theban god often associated with Ra, the sun. He was considered to be the "king of the gods" during the New Kingdom. His temple at Karnak was the largest in all Egypt.

Amulet: object reputed to possess magical powers which protect the wearer.

Anubis: god of funerals, who had embalmed Osiris; he is represented as a wild dog or jackal.

Aten: the divine sun-disk, which became the god of a "monotheistic" religion during the Amarna period.

Bark (sacred or funerary): boats played an essential role in the life of the inhabitants of the Nile valley. They were given a mythical signification, as the vehicle which carried the sun through the underworld. During the burial ceremony, the funerary bark carried the sarcophagus across both the Nile, and the river that separates this world from the next. It figured in the tomb, in the form of either a model or a relief.

Beating out: metalwork technique by which a thin sheet of metal is hollowed out with a hammer. This operation may require the metal to be reheated several times.

Bellows: tool used to produce a stream of air which could be directed onto a fire to make it burn more fiercely. Skins fitted with valves were operated by workers, so that the fires reached the melting point of the metals being processed.

Canopic vase: term deriving from the Greek, for the vases in which the viscera of the deceased were placed after embalming.

Carnarvon, Lord George Herbert (1866-1923): fifth Count of Carnarvon, and Howard Carter's patron during the excavations which led to the discovery of the treasure of Tutankhamun.

Carter, Howard (1873-1939): British Egyptologist who discovered the tomb of Tutankhamun in the Valley of the Kings in 1922.

Cartouche: oval frame, underlined at one end by a bar, in which the name of the pharaoh is inscribed in hieroglyphics. The cartouche is used to frame both the birth name and the royal name of the sovereign, as well as his various titles.

Cavetto cornice: (archit.): concave moulding of circular section, which projects from the top of a wall or a piece of furniture.

Chalcolithic period: (archeol.) age following the neolithic, when copper working techniques were added to those based on polished stone. In Egypt, the chalcolithic began around the middle of the 4th millennium.

Champlevé (relief): bas relief technique projecting from the original surface, as opposed to an incised relief.

Chasing: decorative metalwork technique, using a burin to score the surface.

Clapper ring: jeweller's term for a tube or ring through which the chain on which a pedant or a pectoral hangs is threaded.

Cloisonné: decorative metalwork technique, in which motifs are defined by thin borders standing out from the surface of the object. Fine stones, enamel or coloured glass are then mounted between these borders.

Cobra: the sacred snake of Egypt, representing Wadjyt, the goddess of the Delta. The frieze of cobras that surmounts one of the walls in the Great South Court of Djoser's funerary complex at Saqqara, shows the snakes rearing up: this form is called the uraeus (see below).

Disk (of Aten): the visible form of the sun, worshipped during the heretical reform of Amenophis IV (Akhenaten) to the exclusion of all other gods. This devotion was expressed in, for instance, the "Hymn to the Sun".

Electrum: alloy of gold and silver, long believed by the Egyptians to be a distinct metal in its own right. It occurs naturally in Egypt. It is generally defined as one part gold to seven parts silver.

Ennead: group of nine gods in Egyptian cosmogony.

Ewer: a vase from which water could be poured, usually through a spout. Used in rituals associated with burial rites and ceremonies.

Fields of Iaru (or Fields of Rushes): paradise as it was imagined by the Egyptians in the "Book of the Dead".

Filigree: metalwork technique in which a surface is decorated with arabesques of gold wire fixed to it by soldering. The wire is produced by cutting a thin sheet of metal that has been hammered out into fine strips. When two wires are twisted together, a raised pattern is produced.

Frit (archaeol): vitreous substance, a mixture of silica and coloured oxides, used for glazing blue ceramics. Many shabtis are made from blue-green frit.

Gold: immutable shiny yellow metal, specific gravity 19.3, melts at 1,100 °C (1,945°F), found in Egypt particularly in the mines of Wadi Hammamat.

Granulation, granules: a type of filigree work, made from grains of gold soldered onto a smooth surface (see also: milling).

Hathor: goddess of the heavens, who gave birth to Horus, the sun. She is represented sometimes as a cow, sometimes as a woman. In the Late Period, she was the goddess of the mountain of the dead, and also of joy, of dance and of music. Her emblem is the sistrum.

Hathoric column (Egyptol.): representing the goddess Hathor. Applied to columns or capitals depicting the goddess or one of her emblems.

Hieroglyphs: Ideogrammatical written signs used by the Egyptians, which first appeared in c.3200 BC. They are essentially used for inscriptions on stone monuments and for texts inscribed on metal objects. For everyday writing with brush and ink on papyrus or ostraca, hieratic was used. This is a cursive script, which was in use up till c. 1100 BC. It was then replaced by a simplified cursive script, known as demotic, which survived until the 5th century AD.

Horus: sun god represented as a falcon, and guardian of the king. His principal temple was at Edfu.

Hyksos: an Asiatic people who invaded Egypt at the end of the 13th and beginning of the 14th centuries BC. The chaos they brought with them continued throughout the Second Intermediate Period.

Hypogeum (pl. -ea) (archaeol.): underground tomb, hollowed out of rock.

Inlay: metalwork technique, in which a groove is cut into the surface of a metal object, and a gold or silver wire is set into it with a hammer.

Isis: sister and wife of Osiris, who gathered up the parts of her brother's body after he had been slain by Seth. She then managed to bring him back to life. In this way Osiris became the god of the resurrection of the dead.

Khopri: god who represents the Sun as a child, at the moment of its rising.

Lagide dynasty: Greco-Egyptian royal line, founded by Ptolemy, son of Lagus, in 305 BC, which reigned over Egypt until 30 BC.

Lepsius, Karl Richard (1810-1884): German Egyptologist. During his expedition of 1842-45, he gathered the material for his monumental publication on the Egyptian monuments of Meroë, in the Delta. This work appeared in twelve volumes under the title *Denkmähler aus Ägypten-und Äthiopien* (1849-1859).

Lotus column (archi.): column with a capital in the form of the closed bud of a lotus flower.

Mastaba (Egyptol.): from the Arabic for "bench", it describes a tomb consisting of a vault and a chapel, contained within a low building with sloping walls.

Milling: decoration produced using granulated gold obtained by cutting up gold wire into small sections. When heated, these pieces automatically form into tiny spheres. The granules are then set in place using gum, and fixed there using solder, with the aid of a blow pipe.

Mounting: Setting a stone, a piece of enamel or of glass, by enclosing it within a metal frame.

Naos: a wood or stone construction, which was the Holy of Holies, a temple containing the statue of a god, usually in gold.

Necropolis: from the Greek, "city of the dead": an ancient cemetery.

Niello, niello work: black surface decoration produced using a metallic sulphide, which was heated, then poured molten into a specially prepared space.

Nut: goddess of the heavenly vault. She gave birth to the stars in the dawn of time and, every night, swallowed them, in order to bring them forth again next morning.

Osiris: Egyptian god of vegetation, who later became the god of death and resurrection.

Patera: shallow cup, with no stem, used for libations.

Pectoral: typical Egyptian jewelry, in the form of a pendant, decorated with symbolic motifs. The form may be entirely free, or framed within a trapezoid. Sometimes in openwork, sometimes with cloisonné insets of coloured stone. Its function is both emblematic and protective.

Per-Ramesse: capital built by Ramesses II on the Eastern edge of the Delta, so as to be nearer to the field of battle against the Hittites.

Plating: metalwork technique by which one metal is overlaid with a layer of another more precious metal, to produce for example gilded copper or gilded silver. Save for some small pieces produced by soldering, there is no evidence that the Egyptians practised this technique.

Protohistoric: the period preceding the invention of writing which, in Egypt, is the same as the chalcolithic.

Pschent (Egyptol.): crown of the pharaohs created by uniting the white mitre of Upper Egypt with the red "mortar board" of Lower Egypt. It symbolizes the union of the Two Lands.

Ptah: god of the royal line of Memphis, represented wrapped in a tight sheath of material, like a mummy.

Ptolemies: Rulers of the Greco-Macedonian dynasty which reigned over Egypt from 305 to 30 BC, and whose capital was Alexandria.

Pylon: construction made up of two massive verticals of trapezoidal form, framing the entrance to a temple.

Ramessides: sovereigns of the XIXth and XXth dynasties, who succeeded the short-lived Ramesses I. Under their rule, the land of Egypt flourished, in particular under Sethos I and Ramesses II, in the 14th and 13th centuries BC.

Repoussé: metalworking technique combining hammering and chasing to produce a relief decoration.

Riveting: Process for assembling two pieces of metal, used when it is not possible to solder them. The two sheets of metal are joined together using a rivet, which is a sort of short nail, whose point is flattened out with a hammer where it emerges on the other side.

Rosellini, Ippolito (1800-1843): Italian Egyptologist, friend of Champollion, and author of *Monumenti dell'Egitto e della Nubia*, in 9 volumes (1832-1844).

Saite period: after the town of Sais in the Delta. Defines the period of renaissance that followed the expulsion of the Assyrians by Psamtek I (664-525 BC).

Scarab: beetle which the Egyptians associated with the birth of the sun, by analogy with the ball which the dung-beetle pushes before him. Emblem of resurrection and common subject for amulet designs.

Scroll: decorative motif of curled foliage.

Shabtis (Egyptol.): statuettes made of wood, terracotta, frit or bronze, representing servants and companions of the deceased. Hundreds of them would often be placed in the tomb.

Silver: white metal, specific gravity 10.5, which melts as 960°C (1.860°F). Used by the Egyptians in jewelry, it was very rare for a long time, being imported from Asia Minor. In the Late Period, however, it was also brought from Spain.

Sistrum: Metal or ceramic rattle used to set the rhythm for ritual dances and hymns at the temple. Emblem of Hathor.

Soldering: technique for assembling objects by fusing together two metal surfaces using an alloy whose melting temperature is lower than that of the metals to be joined. Electrum was often used for soldering gold. A solvent, such as borax or pinchbeck could be used to lower the melting point further.

Speos: from the Greek; a cave, temple or tomb set into the rock.

Staining: metalworking technique by which a piece of metal that has been worked already, and annealed or soldered several times, is scoured so as to give it a uniform colour. Ammonia, saltpetre and sea salt are used for this operation.

Swageing: technique for shaping a sheet of metal using a hammer and special anvil known as a swage. Hammering made the part of the sheet that was deformed grow thinner while its surface area spread. By beating the metal in concentric circles, the material that was being forced to the edges could be brought back towards the centre that had been weakened. The ultimate result would be a perfectly spherical curved surface. It was necessary to reheat the object many times during this operation.

Syrinx: from the Greek for flute; term used for gallery tombs drilled into the rock.

Talisman: object possessing magical power to protect its owner and bring him luck.

Tanis: Delta city that was the capital of Egypt from the 11th to the 8th century BC (from the XXIst to the XXIIIrd dynasty).

Triad: in Egyptian cosmogony, a group of three gods composed of a father god, a mother god, and a son god. At Thebes: Amun, Mut and Khonsu; at Edfu: Horus, Hathor and Harsomtus.

Tutankhamun (Tutankhaten): pharaoh of the XVIIIth dynasty (1353-1343) who restored the cult of Amun at Thebes, after the Amarna heresy.

Uraeus: from the Greek *ouraïos*, tail; the rearing cobra who stands guard over the pharaoh, and is often to be found on his crown.

Wadi: dried-up river bed.

Wedjat eye: guardian eye that acts as a talisman, protecting whoever wears it and bringing him strength, according to Egyptian belief.

Plan of Tutankhamun's Tomb

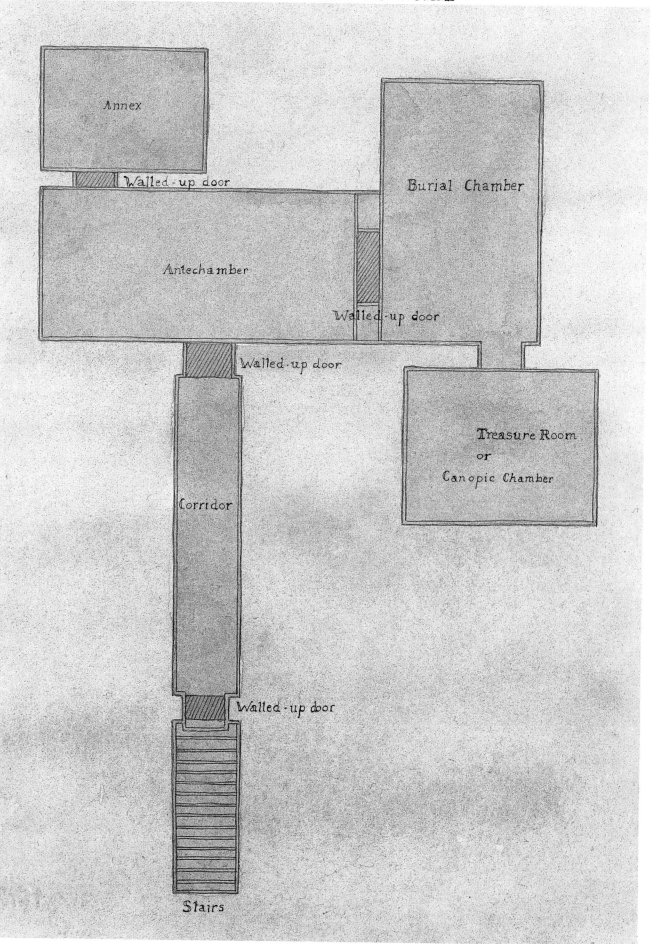

Annex

Burial Chamber

Walled-up door

Antechamber

Walled-up door

Walled-up door

Treasure Room
or
Canopic Chamber

Corridor

Walled-up door

Stairs

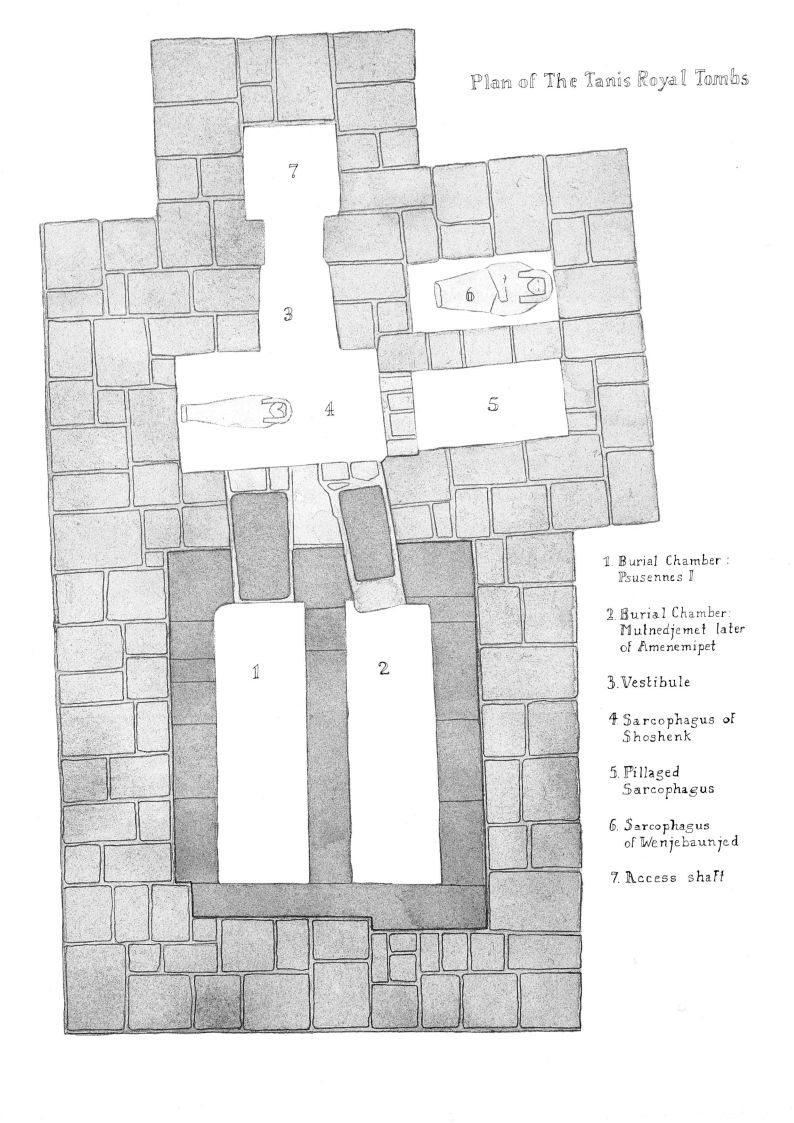

Plan of The Tanis Royal Tombs

1. Burial Chamber:
   Psusennes I

2. Burial Chamber:
   Mutnedjemet later
   of Amenemipet

3. Vestibule

4. Sarcophagus of
   Shoshenk

5. Pillaged
   Sarcophagus

6. Sarcophagus
   of Wenjebaunjed

7. Access shaft

Chronology

PREHISTORY	
Neolithic toward 5500	Agriculture in the Valley of the Nile, first signs of artwork.
Chalcolithic 3500	Nagada: copper smelting and pottery in Lower Egypt.
PREDYNASTIC PERIOD 3200	Monarchy of Buto in Lower Egypt.
FIRST DYNASTIES 3000	Menes unifies the Delta and Upper Egypt: capital Memphis. Thinite Period: Ist and 2nd Dynasties, of kings from Thinis, near Abydos.
2800	Djoser found Third Dynasty at Memphis. Imhotep, Djoser's architect: first pyramid at Saqqara.
OLD KINGDOM 2720	Snoferu founds the Fourth Dynasty at Meydum, pyramid of Meydum and two pyramids of Dahshur.
2690	Kheops: great pyramid of Giza and royal barques.
2660	Khephren: second pyramid of Giza, great sphinx.
2600	Mykerinus: third pyramid of Giza.
2560	Userkaf founds the Fifth Dynasty. *Texts of the Pyramids.*
2420	Teti founds the Sixth Dynasty
2330	Reign of King Pepi II lasts more than ninety years.
FIRST INTERMEDIATE PERIOD 2240	Revolution and upheavals throughout Egypt.
2200	Pillage of the pyramids and tombs of the Old Kingdom. Seventh and Tenth Dynasties at Memphis.
MIDDLE KINGDOM 2050	Reunification and restoration by Mentuhotep I who founds Eleventh Dynasty: capital at Thebes in Upper Egypt. Funerary temple of Deir el-Bahri.
2000	Twelfth Dynasty: capital Lisht in Lower Egypt.
1970	Sesostris I, White Chapel of Karnak.
1785	End of the Twelfth Dynasty.
SECOND INTERMEDIATE PERIOD 1780	Thirteenth and Fourteenth Dynasties: disorders. Hyksos invaders penetrate into the Delta.
1680	Fifteenth and Sixteenth Dynasties of Hyksos rulers. Occupation of Egypt, capital Avaris in the Delta
1600	Independent kingdom at Thebes. Seventeenth Dynasty. Kamosis reconquers Middle Egypt.
NEW EMPIRE 1580	Ahmose expels the Hyksos and founds the Eighteenth Dynasty. Capital in Thebes in Upper Egypt.
1560	Amenophis I.
1530	Tuthmosis I.
1520	Tuthmosis II.
1500	Reign of Queen Hatshepsut with her vizier Senenmut. Temple of Hatshepsut at Deir el-Bahri. Tuthmosis III ascends the throne.
1483	Tomb in the Valley of the Kings.
1450	Amenophis II.

1408	Amenophis III: colossi of Memnon; temple built by royal architect Amenotep-son-of-Hapu; temple of Karnak.
1372	Amenophis IV, the heretic pharaoh who calls himself Akhenaten. Religious crisis. Founds the city of Akhetaten in Tell el-Amarna in Middle Egypt.
1354	Tutankhaten becomes Tutankhamun; capital returns to Thebes.
1343	Reign of King Horemheb. Start of the great hypostyle hall of the Temple of Amun of Karnak.
1314	Ramesses I founds the Nineteenth Dynasty reigning with his son Sethos I. Osireion temple of Abydos. Additions to Temple of Amun at Karnak.
1301	Ramesses II founds new capital of Per-Ramesses in Delta ; Thebes remains religious capital. Completion of hypostyle hall of Temple of Amun at Karnak construction of speos of Abu Simbel and of Ramesseum at Thebes. Tomb of Ramesses II in the Valley of the Kings and end of his 66-year reign.
1235	Dynastic crisis under King Merenptah.
1219	Reigns of Sethos II and Siptah.
1205	Period of disorder; invasions of Libyans and Peoples of the Sea are crushed. Syrian Kings ascend the throne.
1200	Expulsion of foreigners, founding of Twentieth Dynasty.
1198	Reign of Ramesses III; restoration and unification of Egypt. Construction of the Medinet Habu temple.
1168	Decline of the Ramesside kings from the Ramesses IV to IX. High priest Herihor assumes rule of Upper Egypt.
THIRD INTERMEDIATE PERIOD 1085	Smendes founds Twenty-First Dynasty at Tanis in the Delta.
1054	Psusennes I reigns from Tanis.
950	Shoshenq founds the Twenty-Second "Libyan" Dynasty in Tanis.
toward 925	Shoshenq takes Jerusalem and plunders the temple of Solomon.
925	Reign of Osorkon I.
800	Rise to power of the Nubians.
KUSHITE, SAITE AND PERSIAN PERIODS 715	Nubian and Kushite Empires with capitals at Meroe and Napata.
667	Assurbanipal takes Thebes.
663	Psammetichus founds the Twenty-Sixth Dynasty; Saite renaissance.
525	Egypt conquered by a Persian ruler, Cambyses.
378	Nectanebo I founds the Thirtieth Dynasty.
341	Antaxerxes III plunders Egypt.
PTOLEMAIC PERIOD 332	Alexander the Great at Memphis.
331	Foundation of the city of Alexandria.
304	Lagide Dynasty; reign of Ptolemy Soter at Alexandria.
237	Start of the temple of Edfu.
80	Start of the temple of Dendera.
BC 30	End of the Ptolemy lineage.
EGYPT, A ROMAN PROVINCE AD 37	First hypostyle hall of Dendera
41	Hypostyle hall of Esna.
117	Kiosk of Trajan at Philae.
395	Last hieroglyphs at Philae.
470	Last texts in demotic.
550	Closing of the temple of Isis at Philae.

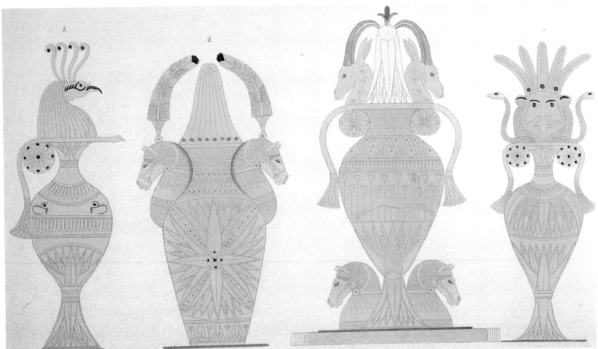

Imaginative excesses in ceremonial goldware

These paintings from the tomb of Ramesses III in the Valley of the Kings, copied with great accuracy by Ippolito Rosellini shortly after 1820, illustrate the extraordinary formal inventiveness shown by Egyptian goldsmiths. These highly-worked gold receptacles were decorated with handles, stems and lids featuring exotic human and animal figures: Nubian slaves, Asiatic prisoners, birds, ibexes and horses, or even snakes. The frescoes offer us a fleeting glimpse of the myriad splendours that must have lain tucked away in the hypogea of the great Ramesside pharaohs, and of which only the slightest fragments have survived.

Acknowledgements

The author and publisher would like to thank the various museums which granted them permission to photograph Egyptian objects and jewels in their collections, and in particular:

the Organization of Egyptian Antiquities, Ministry of Culture, Cairo,

the directors of the Egyptian Museum in Cairo,

the Museum of Egyptian Art in Luxor,

the directors of the Department for Egyptian Antiquities at the Musée du Louvre in Paris,

the directors of the Museo Egizio in Turin.

They would also like to express their gratitude to the directors of the Bibliothèque publique et universitaire, and the Bibliothèque de la Grange, in Geneva, for graciously allowing them to photograph the publications of Rosellini, Champollion, Minutoli, Denon and Lepsius.

All the colour photographs in this book were taken by Anne and Henri Stierlin during visits to Egypt and to various major museums.

The black and white period documents relating to the discovery of the tombs of Tutankhamun and at Tanis have been provided by, respectively, Harry Burton, the Metropolitan Museum of Art, New York (1922-1928), and the Archives of the Keystone Agency/TBG (1939-1940).